Managing With Unions

M. SCOTT MYERS
Center for Applied Management

ADDISON-WESLEY PUBLISHING COMPANY

Reading, Massachusetts • Menlo Park, California
London • Amsterdam • Don Mills, Ontario • Sydney

To the members of local unions—who
ultimately must determine what their
life-style in the workplace is to be.

Contents

Prologue

The Little Red Rooster receives on-the-job training

Once upon a time there was a
Little Red Rooster who scratched about
and uncovered some grains of wheat.

WHO WILL HELP?

He called his barnyard neighbors and said,
"If we work together and plant this wheat,
we will have some fine bread to eat."
"Who will help me plant the wheat?"

After the wheat started growing, the ground turned dry, and there was no rain in sight.

"Who will help me water the wheat?" said the Little Red Rooster.

"Not I," said the Cow.
"I'd lose my workman's compensation," said the Pig.
"Equal rights," said the goose.

"Then I will," said the Little Red Rooster;
and he did.

The wheat grew tall and ripened into golden grain. "Who will help me reap the wheat?" asked the Little Red Rooster.

"I'm waiting for a guaranteed annual wage," said the Cow.
"Out of my classification," said the Pig.
"Not I," said the Goose.

"Then I will," said the Little Red Rooster; and he did.

When it came time to grind
the flour, "Not I," said the Cow.
"I'd lose my unemployment insurance,"
said the Duck.

When it came time to bake the bread,
"That's overtime for me," said the Cow.
"I'm a dropout and never learned how," said the Duck.
"I'd lose my welfare benefits," said the Pig.
"If I'm the only one helping, that's discrimination,"
said the Goose.

"Then I will," said the
Little Red Rooster; and he
did.

He baked five loaves of fine bread and
held them up for his neighbors to see.

"I want some," said the Cow.
"I want some," said the Duck.
"I want some," said the Pig.
"I demand my share," said the Goose.

"No," said the Little Red Rooster,
"I can rest for awhile and eat five
loaves myself."

"Excess profits!" cried the Cow.
"Capitalist leech!" screamed the Duck.
"Company fink!" grunted the Pig.
"Equal rights!" screamed the Goose.

They hurriedly painted picket signs
and marched around the Little Red Rooster,
singing, "We shall overcome."

And they did.

For when the Farmer came to investigate the
commotion, he said, "You must not be greedy,
Little Red Rooster. Look at the oppressed Cow.
Look at the disadvantaged Duck. Look at the
underprivileged Pig. Look at the less fortunate
Goose. You are guilty of making second-class
citizens of them."

"But—but—but I earned the bread," protested the Little Red Rooster.

"Exactly," the wise Farmer said. "That is the wonderful free-enterprise system; anybody in the barnyard can earn as much as he wants. You should be happy to have all this freedom. In other barnyards you would have to give all your loaves to the Farmer. Here you give four loaves to your suffering neighbors."

Prologue

And they lived happily ever after—
including the Little Red Rooster, who
smiled and crowed, "I am grateful, I
am grateful."

But his neighbors wondered why he never
baked any more bread.*

---

*"Wake Up Canada—There's No Free Lunch," *TZ* (Tranair's in-flight magazine), Canadian Federation of Independent Business, Don Mills, Ontario, February 1977, p. 21.

However, the farmer fell on hard times and despaired over the dependency relationship which his farmyard population developed toward him. Moreover, he was facing increasing competition from his neighbors. He recalled wistfully the initiative of Little Red Rooster in the good old days and had an uneasy feeling that he had not responded appropriately to Little Red Rooster's display of initiative. "If only I could recapture that spirit and encourage all members of my farmyard to become the kind of go-getter Little Red Rooster used to be."

Foreword

At one time the basic steel industry of our country was a place of brutalized relationships. Mistrust, suspicion, fear, intimidation, danger, violence, injury, and yes death—such as occurred in the Memorial Day Massacre of 1937 in Chicago—these literally were the hallmarks of America's most basic industry in the days before the United Steelworkers of America.

These conditions were real; people were hurt and killed; and the facts are documented in the history of the times—perhaps most definitively in the reports of the LaFollette Committee on Civil Liberties.

But we were able to build a union—to improve the living standards and the security of our people, to establish a strong organization able to bridge the gap in bargaining power between the individual worker and the huge corporation.

Yes, we of the Steelworkers and the steel companies had our bitter differences in the past, but I believe we came to the point in recent years where we approached problems of mutual concern with all due respect for the integrity of each other.

For example, our union and the ten major basic steel companies agreed to an unprecedented experiment in collective bargaining when we went to the bargaining table early in 1974. The new bargaining procedure was formally called the Experimental Negotiating Agreement (ENA). This new approach to our collective bargaining did not come about with any suddenness.

Back in 1967 we had mutually agreed that we had to solve the twin problems of stockpiling and imports, but we could not agree on the procedure until 1973. Although we agreed in 1967 to seek a new bargaining approach, problems of mutual concern actually began to emerge in the late 1950s, when foreign steel producers started to make inroads on the United States market. The 116-day strike in 1959 provided foreign steel producers an initial opportunity to acquire and cultivate American customers.

From that time on, our problems started to build up each time we went to the bargaining table. During negotiating periods, the market was glutted with more and more imported steel. Meanwhile, the industry kept stepping up production to satisfy the frenzied stockpiling that customers undertook as a hedge against a possible strike. That stockpiling process had its impact not only on our bargaining successes, but also on the ups and downs of production and employment.

Following the 1971 peaceful settlement, many more production units were shut down and complete plants were closed. Some of our members went jobless for more than seven months because of stockpiling that year.

Steel imports in 1971 set an all-time high—18.3 million tons—representing the export of at least 108,000 full-time job opportunities in the American steel industry. The stockpiling and related problems following the 1971 negotiations also cost the ten largest steel makers an estimated $80 million. These harsh economic aftereffects of the 1971 negotiations spurred both sides on with renewed vigor in search for a new bargaining approach. This time our efforts succeeded, and the result was the Experimental Negotiating Agreement used in this year's negotiations.

Briefly, this is what the new bargaining procedure provided: certain, guaranteed minimum benefits for our members, such as at least a three-percent wage hike in each year of the three-year agreement, plus the one-time payment of a bonus of $150 to each member because of the savings the companies would realize from avoiding the effects of stockpiling. Furthermore, it continued our cost-of-living clause, which does not contain a floor or a ceiling.

The new procedure also protected certain existing employee benefits and rights. It safeguarded certain management rights. It allowed the parties to negotiate freely in almost all economic and fringe benefit areas. It eliminated the possibility of an industrywide strike or lockout. It provided for voluntary arbitration of any unresolved bargaining issues. And, for the first time, it gave our local unions the right to strike over local issues. Incidentally, but most importantly, the ENA, before it could be used, had to be approved by the union's Basic Steel Industry Conference, which is made up of presidents of the local unions in the industry, just as it is this Conference that determines the bargaining policy for our negotiations.

The new bargaining procedure worked well in our 1974 negotiations. We reached agreement on a three-year settlement without having to submit one bargainable issue to arbitration. In fact, the ENA worked so well that it was agreed to use the procedure in the 1977 negotiations, and again an overall settlement was reached without resort to the arbitration procedure, and it was agreed to use ENA in the 1980 talks.

In my opinion, we made labor-management history when we used ENA initially in 1974. For the first time, we concluded a complete, major settlement in a critical industry without the threat of an industrywide strike or lockout. This—to me—was a new, revolutionary event in the collective bargaining process, because until then it had been assumed that no equitable settlement of this magnitude could possibly be concluded without the threat of brute force dominating the talks.

The new bargaining procedure that we helped pioneer establishes the fact that it is possible, without brandishing the threat of a national work stoppage, to negotiate agreements as effective as when the traditional weapons of labor and management are present at the bargaining table. The basic ingredient is a determination and a commitment by *both* sides to engage in good-faith bargaining.

I do not endorse everything that Scott Myers has written in this book, but to the extent that it represents a continuing effort on his part to further the kind of labor-management relationship that led to the use of the Experimental Negotiating Agreement in the basic steel industry, I commend him for his efforts.

I. W. Abel, President
United Steelworkers of America,
1965-1977

Preface
and Acknowledgments

An effective organization satisfies two basic human conditions:

1. Its members are free to assert themselves as individuals, and
2. Its members are united in the pursuit of common goals.

Because these two conditions are inherently or potentially in conflict, their satisfaction requires a delicate balance between them. These conditions are not easily attainable in a unionized organization, as a unionized work force is usually an organization divided against itself.

However, these conditions may be satisfied in a unionized organization if the company and union are not competing with each other for the allegiance of their common members. Dual, or lopsided, allegiance to adversaries is self-defeating to the adversary groups and their members, but dual allegiance to allies is conducive to the pursuit of mutually supportive goals.

In 1976 the National Center for Productivity and Quality of Working Life published a 94-page booklet entitled *Recent Initiatives in Labor-Management Cooperation*. Examples in this booklet are similar to, though not as detailed as, case studies described in a 383-page book entitled *Causes of Industrial Peace Under Collective Bargaining*, published in 1955 under the sponsorship of the National Planning Association.* These publications are descriptive of union-management collaboration in recent decades—some of them extending back one-half century.

Company-union relationships described in these publications and observed in contemporary organizations may be characterized in terms of three models:

1. *Model 1—Win-Lose Adversary.* This is the traditional model based on adversary relationships between company and union, in

---

*Clinton S. Golden and Virginia D. Parker, *Causes of Industrial Peace Under Collective Bargaining*, New York: Harper and Brothers, 1955.

which political, economic, and legal pressures prevail, and company and union display little or no sensitivity to their symbiotic relationships and common goals.

2. *Model 2—Collaborative Adversary.* Company and union unite to improve quality of life, cost effectiveness, productivity, conflict resolution, and other conditions peripheral to pay, benefits, job security, and other central issues of collective bargaining. However, the company and union coexist under conditions of détente, preserving mutually exclusive management prerogatives and labor rights and the basic two-class system.

3. *Model 3—Industrial Democracy.* Company and union operate from a common data base in a climate of mutual trust to achieve joint-stake organizational objectives. Managers and union officials minimize the use of official authority and broaden the interactive role of people in all levels and functions to include solving problems, setting goals, evaluating organizational effectiveness, and designing systems for utilizing, developing, and compensating themselves.

Most of the cases described in the two publications noted above are examples of movement from Model 1 to Model 2. Encouraging as this transition may be, Model 2 represents a half-way house on the road to industrial democracy. Underlying Model 2 collaboration is a persevering assumption that management and labor are inherently two distinct classes whose conflicting goals are made more bearable by an armed truce of peaceful coexistence.

However, the Model 2 case studies described in the more recent publication are more likely to evolve to Model 3 than those in the 1955 publication, because of four fundamental reasons:

1. Contemporary union members are more enlightened than their counterparts of earlier eras and are more responsive to opportunity for self-actualization and less tolerant of domination by company and union authority figures.

2. Union leaders are also more enlightened and recognize the limitations of wages, hours, and working conditions for satisfying the needs of their more enlightened constituency. Though somewhat uneasy about the increasing ambiguity of their time-honored adversary charter, more union officers are willing to explore their changing role in the pursuit of industrial democracy.

3. Company managers are more sophisticated in principles of motivation and are encouraging the constructive expression of talent as the only viable alternative to counterproductive rebellion. Today's managers have fewer hang-ups than their predecessors with needs for managerial prerogatives and rank-oriented status symbols.

4. Trends in legislation and corporate innovations are encouraging the broader implementation of total systems sharing plans such as employee stock ownership, profit sharing, and Scanlon-type plans. Such systems, in combination with improved work-life processes, tend to depolarize the management-labor dichotomy.

The purpose of *Managing With Unions* is to facilitate the evolution of labor relations toward Models 2 and 3, recognizing that Model 2 is not a terminal goal, but a necessary transitional stage on the way to industrial democracy.

I am indebted to John A. Paré for many ideas presented in this book. His leadership and personal skill in converting company-union confrontation into collaborative effort has accelerated the understanding and acceptance of union-management cooperation in the United States and Canada.

The Work in American Institute and the National Center for Productivity and Quality of Working Life are having a powerful influence in furthering the cause and processes for pursuing industrial democracy.

I am indebted to the innovative managers and union members who have risked their personal and professional status to pioneer in the conversion of traditional adversary relationship to one of collaboration.

My wife, Susan, has contributed indirectly to the preparation of this book through her involvement in the union-company workshops on which Chapters 4, 5, and 6 are based. She has improved the total manuscript directly by influencing the content and through editorial refinements.

Coral Gables, Florida   M.S.M.
March 1978

List of Exhibits

Chapter 1

The Changing Society

Viewed from the uncontaminated perspective of a visitor from outer space, labor relations as commonly practiced in democratic societies would represent a paradox. The paradox is the caste system unwittingly created by a process presumed to have democratic underpinnings.

Labor unions were created to protect people from exploitation and to support the democratic cornerstone of a "government of the people, by the people, for the people." Early union leaders were influenced by Karl Marx's vision of a classless society evolving from the organized proletariat successfully suppressing the exploitive bourgeoisie. Apparently Marx and his disciples did not anticipate the eventual role of the organized proletariat (labor unions) in widening and crystallizing the gap between the upper and lower classes and artificially perpetuating their adversary relationships. Nor did Marx appear to understand that the enlightened bourgeoisie would discover exploitation to be self-defeating and for business (not altruistic) reasons convert to industrial democracy.

The polarization of management and labor has established tangible boundaries for the proletariat which, despite their economic victories, have firmly entrenched them in a class identity, pitted against their defensively united fellow citizens, who are also identifiable by exclusive class distinctions. Traditional labor relations philosophy has influenced management and labor alike to regard each other as natural enemies, necessarily though warily united in a symbiotic relationship. In this necessary, though adversary, alliance, management's role is to act, and labor's role is to react. Implicit in this relationship is the notion that labor is ever ready to act as the conscience of a management whose behavior otherwise would be exploitively self-serving.

So firmly entrenched is the union's watch-dog role and its assumptions about management that altruistic acts on the part of management are generally presumed to be inspired by ulterior motives. Management, in turn, is similarly conditioned to oppose union initiative on the assumption that labor is bent on eroding managerial prerogatives and accelerating the

1

infiltration of creeping socialism. Hence management and labor are each imprisoned in roles created and perpetuated by their assumptions about each other.

The union-management relationship was crystallized during an era in early America when workers were struggling at subsistence levels and many employers were indeed exploitive. The focus of collective bargaining was on wages, hours, and working conditions—portrayed in Exhibit 1 as maintenance needs. However, during the past century, as these lower-order needs gradually became better satisfied, people had a natural readiness to move psychologically upward to satisfy higher-order self-actualization, or motivation, needs in terms of growth, achievement, responsibility, and recognition. But the union, in the interest of protecting people against exploitation, unwittingly deprived wage earners of the opportunity to satisfy their higher-order needs by narrowly circumscribing their job duties. Union charters and labor laws have gradually coalesced to define labor as people who work with their hands and management as people who work with their heads. In effect, members of labor are customarily paid for the number of hours their bodies are on the job, whereas members of management are more typically paid for their creative accomplishments.

Thus although the union has been successful in counteracting economic oppression, in its place it has unintentionally substituted a far more oppressive type of mental impoverishment.

ORIGIN OF THE TWO-CLASS SYSTEM

The management-labor adversary relationship is an extension of the two-class system traceable to the dawn of history. Ancient history makes reference to master-slave and landlord-serf relationships. Royalty-commoner and officer-soldier are enduring manifestations of prehistoric two-class systems. In the Middle Ages the journeyman-apprentice relationship gradually evolved with capitalism and the Industrial Revolution to the management-labor dichotomy which characterizes labor relations in most modern organizations.

The two-class system is largely a function of discrepancies between the upper and lower classes in terms of two fundamental criteria—knowledge and wealth. Generally speaking, members of the upper class have had more knowledge and wealth than members of the lower class. Knowledge, as it is used in this context, refers to the body of knowledge officially accepted by the ruling class. Thus the religion of the ruling class of the Middle Ages may not always have passed the test of rational scrutiny, but it was the official body of knowledge that justified the suppression of infidels, no matter how scientifically rational the dissenters may have been. Knowledge, to be acceptable, must fit the norms of the day. Socrates, for example, was ahead of his time and was forced to give up his life because his knowledge challenged the accepted wisdom of the ruling class. However, in most cases the

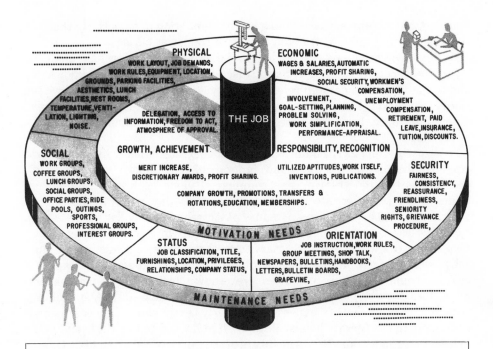

PHYSICAL
WORK LAYOUT, JOB DEMANDS, WORK RULES, EQUIPMENT, LOCATION, GROUNDS, PARKING FACILITIES, AESTHETICS, LUNCH FACILITIES, REST ROOMS, TEMPERATURE, VENTILATION, LIGHTING, NOISE.

DELEGATION, ACCESS TO INFORMATION, FREEDOM TO ACT, ATMOSPHERE OF APPROVAL.

THE JOB

ECONOMIC
WAGES & SALARIES, AUTOMATIC INCREASES, PROFIT SHARING, SOCIAL SECURITY, WORKMEN'S COMPENSATION, UNEMPLOYMENT COMPENSATION, RETIREMENT, PAID LEAVE, INSURANCE, TUITION, DISCOUNTS.

INVOLVEMENT, GOAL-SETTING, PLANNING, PROBLEM SOLVING, WORK SIMPLIFICATION, PERFORMANCE-APPRAISAL.

GROWTH, ACHIEVEMENT
MERIT INCREASE, DISCRETIONARY AWARDS, PROFIT SHARING.

RESPONSIBILITY, RECOGNITION
UTILIZED APTITUDES, WORK ITSELF, INVENTIONS, PUBLICATIONS.

SOCIAL
WORK GROUPS, COFFEE GROUPS, LUNCH GROUPS, SOCIAL GROUPS, OFFICE PARTIES, RIDE POOLS, OUTINGS, SPORTS, PROFESSIONAL GROUPS, INTEREST GROUPS.

COMPANY GROWTH, PROMOTIONS, TRANSFERS & ROTATIONS, EDUCATION, MEMBERSHIPS.

SECURITY
FAIRNESS, CONSISTENCY, REASSURANCE, FRIENDLINESS, SENIORITY RIGHTS, GRIEVANCE PROCEDURE,

MOTIVATION NEEDS

STATUS
JOB CLASSIFICATION, TITLE, FURNISHINGS, LOCATION, PRIVILEGES, RELATIONSHIPS, COMPANY STATUS,

ORIENTATION
JOB INSTRUCTION, WORK RULES, GROUP MEETINGS, SHOP TALK, NEWSPAPERS, BULLETINS, HANDBOOKS, LETTERS, BULLETIN BOARDS, GRAPEVINE,

MAINTENANCE NEEDS

Effective job performance depends on the fulfillment of both motivation and maintenance needs. Motivation needs include growth, achievement, responsibility, and recognition and are satisfied primarily through the media grouped in the inner circle. They focus on the individual and his or her achievement of company and personal goals.

Maintenance needs are satisfied through media listed in the outer circle under the headings of physical, social, status, orientation, security, and economic. Peripheral to the task and usually group-administered, maintenance factors have little motivational value, but their fulfillment is essential to the avoidance of dissatisfaction. An environment rich in opportunities for satisfying motivation needs leads to motivation-seeking habits; a job situation sparse in motivation opportunities encourages preoccupation with maintenance factors and the development of maintenance seekers.

In other words, in a situation of satisfied motivation needs, maintenance factors have relatively little influence as either satisfiers or dissatisfiers. However, the removal of opportunity for meaningful achievement sensitizes the individual to his or her environment, and perception of maintenance factors becomes colored by a readiness to find fault.

Thus motivation, or the achievement of personal goals, is not facilitated by management actions which emphasize maintenance media, but rather by actions which provide balanced opportunity for the satisfaction of both motivation and maintenance needs.

Exhibit 1 Employee needs—motivation and maintenance.*

knowledge of the upper classes had a better foundation in objectivity than the superstition and folklore-oriented beliefs of the lower classes.

The two-class system tended to be self-perpetuating, as moneyed members of society had the means and discretionary time to pursue knowledge and to qualify for leadership roles in society, government, the military, the clergy, education, and commerce. The lower class, continuously preoccupied with subsistence, had little time or opportunity to gain membership in the upper class.

In early America the blue-collar worker characteristically lived in a world circumscribed by oppression and ignorance. The label "working stiff" accurately reflected the worker's commercial value as brawn rather than brain. Child labor, eighteen-hour days, and six-day work weeks were a worker's normal expectations. Because pay rates of blue-collar workers were typically less than one-fourth the pay levels of white-collar workers, long hours and work weeks were necessary to meet subsistence needs. Many blue-collar workers were illiterates or immigrants with language handicaps. Of course, communication media as we know them today—newspapers, magazines, moving pictures, telephones, radio, television—and easy mobility were not part of the life experience of early Americans. Indeed, reading experience in the literate household was often limited to the Bible and other moralistic publications. Hence members of the working class had little time or energy to pursue life enrichment, nor would they, with their circumscribed perspective, know what to pursue if given the opportunity. It was not unusual for clergymen of that era to explain human suffering as the consequence of, and atonement for, original sin. Hence many oppressed workers accepted their lot in life as though it were the natural order of things as prescribed by the deity—going to their ultimate deaths never realizing that they were the victims of a giant deception.

EMERGENCE OF THE ADVERSARY RELATIONSHIP

The two-class system was in full force in early America before the influence of labor legislation and collective bargaining began ameliorating the situation of exploited wage earners. When Samuel Gompers and other crusaders for social and economic justice launched their unionization efforts in the latter part of the nineteenth century, they based their strategies on the assumption that management and labor have differing and contradictory goals. In his 1898 presidential report to the Convention of the American Federation of Labor, Gompers stated: "Trade unions. . .were born of the necessity of the workers to protect and defend themselves from encroachment, injustice and wrong."* The Constitution of the Industrial Workers of the World (IWW), founded in

---

*Florence Calvert Thorne, *Samuel Gompers—American Statesman,* New York: Philosophical Library, 1957, p. 17.

1905 by William Haywood, stated: "The working class and the employing class have nothing in common. . . . Between these two classes a struggle must go on until the workers of the world organize as a class, take possession of the earth and the machinery of production, and abolish the wage system. . . . It is the historic mission of the working class to do away with capitalism." Gompers, Haywood, and other early union leaders didn't create the two-class system; they merely described the reality existing in early America and had the insight and temerity to lead a revolt against industrial tyranny.

Labor legislation and collective bargaining gradually began ameliorating the plight of the working person. A third force—mass-production technology—simultaneously began pricing more goods within reach of wage earners, thereby upgrading the quality of life of the worker's family. Unfortunately, mass-production work systems tended to limit the constructive expression of talent and initiative and therefore had adverse psychological impact on worker job satisfaction and productivity. Frustrated workers, now working under constraints imposed by well-meaning labor laws and unions, began expressing their talents in counterproductive pursuits, thereby undermining much of the anticipated gains of mass-production technology.

THE WORKER'S CHANGING PERSPECTIVE

As workers' pay escalated and their leisure time increased, they were psychologically ready to move, in their needs hierarchy, from subsistence or maintenance needs to higher-order needs for growth, achievement, responsibility, and recognition. By 1950 workers' horizons were broadened and their self-awareness deepened by a multiplicity of media. Many workers had just returned from far-flung involvement in World War II with a more cosmopolitan perspective and, at an accelerated pace, were gaining access to radio, television, newspapers, periodicals, movies, and jet aircraft in a society of increasing secularism and paternalism.

Television undoubtedly had the greatest single impact on the perceptions of the working person. During the 1950s television became available to almost any American who wanted it. TV antennae sprouted on the roofs of ghetto shanties as quickly as they appeared on the custom-built homes of the upper classes. By the early '70s, 97 percent of American homes had one or more TV sets.

When television was new, members of the lower socioeconomic strata tended to watch cartoons, comedies, and westerns, whereas the preferences of the more formally educated leaned more toward newscasts, fine arts, and other educational programs. However, many lower-class members soon tired of slapstick fare and began watching a wider variety of programs. Many began finding educational programs interesting, due in part to the fact that no authority figure told them they were "educational." Hence program preferences of viewers in all classes gradually began coalescing toward a common fare.

5

ADVERSARIES SHARE A DATA BASE

For the first time in known human history, people of all classes were being influenced by a common data base. Class differences in viewing preferences diminished as television began gradually raising the knowledge level of the culturally disadvantaged toward the level of the formally educated. Though differing substantially in years of formal education, workers and managers began drifting toward common perceptions and values. Indeed, the younger workers entering the work force were sometimes more liberal, worldly, and sophisticated than their supervisors. But the younger workers had spent more of their life in front of TV sets than had their supervisors, who were more strongly oriented toward the pursuit of career goals. Thus supervisors who acquired their leadership roles by industriousness, loyalty, and manipulation were less well educated in some respects than the "ungrateful wretches" who entered the work force seemingly with low commitment, cynicism, and unrealistic expectations.

The deterioration of the old work ethic was not simply a function of exposure to TV, of course, but was also a result of the impact of other media and selective perception arising from a combination of parental permissiveness, societal paternalism, reaction to materialism, and peer pressure. The interaction of these factors in an affluent and relief-oriented society did much to emasculate the Horatio Alger theory that one succeeded through hard work, honesty, ambition, perseverence, sacrifice, and loyalty. It was a case of incomplete or distorted information dispensed by TV, lean on economics, civics, and sociology and heavy on commercials and programs fostering and appealing to hedonism. Thus the new generation came into the organizations inadequately oriented to pursue a full life of responsible citizenship as it was envisioned and prescribed by earlier generations.

CLOSURE OF THE KNOWLEDGE AND MONEY GAP

Despite this distortion or incompatibility in life orientation, workers in the new generation were in some respects better informed than many of the supervisors on whom they depended for self-actualization in the workplace. Though their supervisors might be better oriented toward the economics and politics of survival and success in the workplace, they often embraced a set of unflattering assumptions about people and how they should be motivated. Theory X, rather than Theory Y assumptions (see Chapter 4), tended to be the foundation for managerial practice. However, the managers were in power, and in exercising their official, though self-defeating, prerogatives, they continued to use persuasion, bribery, manipulation, and threats to get the "ungrateful wretches" to shape up and get in step. But, of course, official "boss power" was now matched by unofficial "people power," made official by the charters of labor unions.

Along with the closure of the knowledge gap noted above came a reduction in the income gap between management and labor. Largely through legislation and collective bargaining, blue-collar wages gradually rose to the level of the white-collar workers'. Indeed, by the early '70s, it was not uncommon to encounter first-line supervisors taking home smaller pay checks than the people they supervised.

Thus, at last, the blue-collar worker is essentially both as well informed and as well paid as the white-collar worker. Now, as never before, the psychological and economic conditions are right for converting the adversary relationships between management and labor into collaboration. The concepts of management prerogatives and labor rights are now understood to be self-defeating. Were it not for the power of long-term cultural conditioning, the mutually exclusive definitions of management and labor could be easily obliterated.

THE PERSEVERING PARENT TAPES

Unfortunately, the win-lose, management-labor cleavage and its correlates left indelible imprints on the minds of the contestants. The Parent tapes of managers are still programmed in terms of management prerogatives with Parent-Child strategies for maximizing performance by manipulating company resources, particularly its people.* The Parent tapes of hourly paid workers and their union leaders are just as strongly programmed to react to authority and to exercise Child-Parent strategies to "get away with" doing as little as possible. Thus we find well-informed members of management and labor potentially capable of synergizing their pursuits of common goals, but instead unwittingly victimizing themselves by perpetuating tradition in the pursuit of mutually exclusive goals.

Labor laws and the strategies of labor relations built around them also create and perpetuate the two-class system. For instance, the National Labor Relations Act (NLRA) describes a supervisor as a person whose job requires the exercise of independent judgment and who has the authority to hire, transfer, suspend, lay off, recall, promote, discharge, assign, reward, or discipline employees. Employees, in contrast, are described in terms which imply their exemption from the use of independent judgment and from influencing the conduct of other employees. Unlike supervisors, employees have the right to form and join labor unions and to engage in collective bargaining. In other words, the usual interpretation of the NLRA establishes a parent-child relationship between supervisors and employees. Though the NLRA was enacted to protect people from exploitation, one of its unintended impacts has been to circumscribe the self-expression of employees who, in many well-run organizations, do in fact exercise independent judgment and in various ways influence the productivity and conduct of their peers.

Jules J. Justin, through his prestigious Industrial Relations Workshop Seminars and publications, is representative of the consultants who have

---

*See pp. 59-61 for definition of Parent, Adult, and Child personality components.

shaped labor relations strategy in the United States and Canada. With regard to the role of employees as influenced by unions, Justin holds that the union cannot join with management in managing:

> **Rule 7:** THE UNION CANNOT COOPERATE WITH MANAGEMENT IN MANAGING THE EMPLOYEES. THE SHOP STEWARD CANNOT CO-OPERATE WITH THE SUPERVISOR IN SUPERVISING THEM. *

> . . . . even in the area of safety, unions cannot join with management in managing. Everyone believes in safety. But when an employee violates a safety rule and his supervisor disciplines him, the shop steward defends the employee! He must. That's his job. He can't take disciplinary responsibility unto himself, for he "would surely be chastised at the next union meeting and defeated at the next election." The shop steward's office compels him to defend the employee and try to win his case, good or bad!

> Unions can no more cooperate with management in enforcing safe practices or assume disciplinary responsibilities for an employee violating established safety rules than they can join with management in making the workers toe the line or increase efficiency. That's your worry, Mr. Supervisor!†

Moreover, Dr. Justin conveys an unflattering charter for the union:

> From top to bottom the union constitutes a political body. Inside and outside the work unit the union exists, functions, operates and survives as a political organism. The fact that the union functions as a political organization does not detract from its status. I do not suggest anything wrong or bad but only that a union differs from a business organization in its motives, in its goals, and in how it acts to achieve its goals.‡

To the extent that labor relations directors operate from these assumptions, management-labor conflict is a self-fulfilled prophecy.

For many, the management-labor polarization is as deeply ingrained as religious orientation, mentioned later. Like religious identity, class identity is programmed by countless impressions, both vivid and subtle, throughout a lifetime, but particularly during the formative years of youth. For example, the business suit and the hard hat, or white collar and blue collar, are symbols of class identity which condition young, impressionable minds and, of course, reinforce crystallized attitudes.

Exhibit 2 illustrates the variety of criteria in society which historically had distinguished management from labor. In each of the 54 pairs, the management-associated term appears on the left and the labor term on the right. These criteria are not absolute, of course, but in the aggregate reflect

---

*Jules J. Justin, *How to Manage with a Union*, Book One, New York: Industrial Relations Workshop Seminars, 1969, p. 19.

†*Ibid.*, p. 18.

‡*Ibid.*, p. 6.

Exclusive homes/tract homes	Progress reports/time clocks
Having servants/being servants	Bonuses/overtime pay
Steak/hamburger	Stock options/piece-work incentives
New automobiles/used cars	Tax shelters/payroll deductions
Lincoln Continental/Chevrolet	Dining room/brown bag
Mercedes/Volkswagen	Leisurely lunches/hurried lunches
Stylish clothing/work clothing	Company person/union member
Department stores/discount stores	Giving orders/receiving orders
Taxis/subways	Private offices/work stations
Airplane trips/auto trips	Engineers/mechanics
Summer camps/summer jobs	Professional society/labor union
Country clubs/public parks	Management meetings/union rallies
Fawning teachers/frowning teachers	Society conventions/union conven-
Helpful policemen/menacing police-	tions
men	Sabbatical leave/change of jobs
College aspirations/trade school orien-	Honoraria/moonlighting
tation	Afternoon golfing/evening bowling
College graduates/high school drop-	Summer cottages/motels and campers
outs	Classical music/country-western
Barber shops/home haircuts	Pianos and violins/guitars and banjos
Orthodontics/dental neglect	Broadway plays/local movies
Paying cash/installment buying	Cocktail parties/beer busts
Bank accounts/hoarded cash	Original paintings/multilith reproduc-
Credit cards/cash	tions
My Dad is smarter/my Dad is tougher	Four Seasons/McDonald's
Clean hands/dirty hands	Neiman Marcus/Sears
Coat and tie/open-neck shirt	Episcopalians/Baptists
Briefcases/lunch pails	Republicans/Democrats
Salary/wages	*Saturday Review/National Enquirer*
Job security/layoff vulnerability	

Exhibit 2 Correlates of the American two-class system.

the many dimensions of the labor-management dichotomy. So indelibly ingrained was this class identity that should happenstance suddenly endow a member of the lower class with money, this *nouveau-riche* person might still be rejected by the closed fraternity of the established upper class. This rejection occurs not solely because of the person's humble origin, but perhaps more so because his or her life-style—intellectually, philosophically, politically, socially, and economically—was toward the lower class.

These correlates of class distinction collectively have shaped images which impede the unfreezing of class identity. However, the mass media, in bridging the knowledge gap between classes, have served as a mirror, enabling workers to begin understanding who they are and what they would like to have and to become. With their appetites whetted by TV commercials and self-awareness, they began seeking the advantages and symbols of upper-class membership such as credit cards, checking accounts, country clubs, orthodontics, airplane trips, piano lessons, expensive restaurants, luxurious autos, and college educations. Thus members of the working class are increasingly ready, intellectually and attitudinally, to bridge the gap of social distance in the workplace and community.

However, members of the upper class rarely seek the obliteration of class distinctions with the same zeal as do the workers, particularly in older societies. To the contrary, some members of the upper class see the improving status of the worker as an encroachment on their territory and as the erosion of their valued class distinctions. The diminishing vestiges of gold spittoons, executive dining rooms, and other upper-class security blankets evoke increasing tenacity and defensiveness on the part of those who desire to preserve this two-class system.

But not all members of the upper class value the traditional symbols of upper-class membership. By a curious twist of circumstances, many who would be entitled by heritage, wealth, or vocational role to flaunt symbols of their higher status are symbolically rejecting the traditional life-style of the ruling class. This trend is particularly true of, but not restricted to, the younger generation. Many enlightened youths have rebelled against their parents' status quo politics, conservative clothing, exclusive socializing, and 1939 hair styles and have adopted the clothing, social norms, politics, and hair styles previously associated with the culturally disadvantaged. Hence gradually, sometimes rebelliously or defiantly, the grey-flannel-suit syndrome is abandoned in favor of blue jeans, sneakers, long hair, and informality. It has become increasingly difficult to establish class identity on the basis of appearance or social and political orientation. In fact, ambitious members of the working class sometimes display more of the traditional symbols of upper-class membership than management-class members do themselves. Diamond Jim Brady's philosophy of "Them as has 'em wears 'em" is attracting fewer adherents in today's society.

Organizational inertia sometimes prevents the abolishment of class-oriented status symbols in the workplace at the pace that society as a whole is rejecting them. Indeed, the rank-oriented class standards of the workplace continue to inhibit the expression of democracy in the community. For instance, the long-term, close-neighbor friendship of two oil refinery technicians and their respective families was disrupted when one who was promoted into supervision brought home his new white hard hat, symbol of membership in management.

To a great extent, the philosophy of a total culture is shaped by the managerial styles and systems in the workplaces of that culture. Democratic or autocratic behavior in the organization is often subtly transferred into the home, to nurture democracy and mutual respect or autocracy and hostility. Children passing through adolescence and adulthood in these homes move into parental and occupational roles which perpetuate the values and practices which guided their own maturation. Hence, in a circular fashion, life-styles in the community are influenced by social norms in the organization. If the adversary two-class system is to be eradicated, deliberate strategies are needed in the workplace to complement cultural-reconditioning trends in the total society.

A PARALLEL IN RELIGION

The adversary relationship between company and union is an understandable, though unnecessary, extension of the two-class system described earlier. However, converting adversary relationships to collaboration is not a viable proposition to be achieved simply by edict, legislation, evangelism, or even as a result of the sincere resolutions of the involved adversaries. This conversion process is no less difficult than the conversion of the members of one religion to membership in another.

Consider, for example, the feasibility of converting Protestants in Ireland to Catholicism, or Christians in Lebanon to Islam, or Moslems in Iran to Judaism. Such conversions are not impossible, as they are occurring continuously on a small scale. Over a long period of time, significant shifts in religious orientation have taken place. For instance, Buddhism is no longer found in India, its birthplace, having been gradually displaced by other religions. However, it has slowly won converts in other countries. Broad-scale conversions such as this require two basic conditions: (1) widespread dissatisfaction with the status quo, and (2) the existence of viable alternatives.

In other words, individuals leave their religion and adopt another only if they see an advantage in such a conversion. For example, some convert to acquire individual or group acceptance, such as a condition of marriage; some to enhance career opportunity; others to escape social, economic, or political ostracism; some as a result of an emotional experience; some to follow a charismatic leader; some as a result of occult revelations. A few convert to avoid or to seek the responsibility of self-reliance. Whatever the reasons, persons who become committed to a new psychological position usually must overcome the deep-seated conditioning which oriented them to their previous position. The emotional underpinnings of a value system crystallized during the formative years cannot be simply cast aside by an intellectual insight. Hence some converts ultimately revert to their previous position, particularly when their intellectual rebellion encounters the regressive influence of senility. This backsliding may occur gradually as the attractions of conversion are gradually outweighed by enduring influences of their earlier conditioning, or it may occur suddenly as a result of emotional stress which causes them to regress to an earlier psychological level.

However, children of the convert, who begin their acculturation process early, may reach adulthood fully oriented to their parents' acquired religion and would not normally or easily abandon this orientation except for some of the reasons mentioned above. Thus in the time required for the members of one generation to replace their parents, the conversion may be complete. Descendants of this second generation rationalize and perpetuate their religion as a matter of course through their descendants, blindly defending it when "outsiders" attack it. Ultimately, it is not their religion that is at stake, but rather their group, their religion being merely the basis for group identity. Thus the friction between Moslems and Christians or between Moslems and Jews in the Middle East, for example, is not caused by incompatibility of religion, but rather by issues peripheral to religious beliefs. However, religious orientation becomes a convenient criterion for drawing tangible battle lines for economic, social, and political discrimination, and these in turn are the real issues over which battles are fought.

Occasionally, during the evolution of a culture, a religious framework may be perceived as inadequate for, or a detriment to, coping with widespread societal problems. In this case, large segments of the population become candidates for mass conversion. Thus in the Middle Ages, when the Catholic church seemed inadequate for ameliorating the exploitation spawned by the new capitalism, the time was ripe for Martin Luther and John Calvin to protest the status quo and to offer a religion of self-determination and self-reliance. The Protestant ethic became such a powerful influence in North America that its tenets permeated the total culture for Protestants and non-Protestants alike.

The Protestant ethic originally compelled people to succeed in life to earn a place in Heaven or to prove to themselves and the world that they were destined for salvation. As the religious underpinnings of the work ethic were gradually forgotten, the compulsion to work remained as its own virtue. Hence ambition, perseverance, thrift, sacrifice, loyalty, and progress all came to be adjectives of virtue in early America. This theme was captured, reinforced, and perpetuated by writers such as Horatio Alger, whose novels reflected and made credible the American dream of "rags to riches." Typical Parent tapes of the era were:

An idle mind is the Devil's workshop.

A stitch in time saves nine.

Don't put off till tomorrow what you can do today.

Early to bed, early to rise, makes a man healthy, wealthy and wise.

A penny saved is a penny earned.

If at first you don't succeed, try, try again.

Practice makes perfect.

Now the entrepreneurial and materialistic Protestant ethic, which both supported and was supported by the Industrial Revolution, is becoming increasingly incompatible with new values evolving in mass-media societies. Many people who are products of today's affluent and well-informed cultures are less concerned with economic security and symbols of status than they are with quality of life and other existential issues. The virtue of work itself, with its traditional demands for obedience and gratitude, has little appeal to many newcomers to the work force.

The religious orientation of individuals and groups and how these orientations have been altered is a model for understanding the reconditioning process to be activated if people are to escape the win-lose entrapments caused by the management-labor dichotomy. The union-management polarization has roots fully as well established as religious orientations. And like religions, these may be uprooted if attractive alternatives are available. However, people who rebel against traditional labor relations are continuously vulnerable to backsliding, but the new generations, programmed with new tapes, are intellectually and emotionally ready for democracy in the workplace.

Klaus Offermann, fork lift driver at Kootenay Forest Products, is representative of this new generation. His paper, reproduced in Appendix B, is a reflection of the readiness of many contemporary workers to be responsibly involved in productivity and other aspects of organizational health.

INDUSTRIAL DEMOCRACY

Conditions that abolish the two-class system are referred to in this book as "industrial democracy." This term is not restricted to industry, but may apply equally in the public sector or any place of employment. Democracy does not imply permissiveness or management by majority, but rather any goal-oriented subsociety in which individuals at work maintain their individuality while synergistically pursuing common goals. Industrial democracy is not synonymous with socialism or a classless society. Classifications will always exist and are not detrimental when they are the consequences of free choice. A person's membership in a given class or status group tends to be oppressive when such membership is a result of regimentation and is inescapable. For example, requirements such as punching a time clock, exclusion from a parking lot or executive dining room, and restrictive dress codes, all enforced by official authority, function as social barriers to escape of second-class citizenship. These conditions and other rank-oriented status symbols increase social distance and hence are barriers to communication

However, exclusive class distinctions or group memberships, particularly if they are manifestations of free choice, need not be detrimental to democracy. Indeed, they might be the essence of democracy. Away from the job, for example, memberships in bowling leagues, tennis clubs, square dance groups, school boards, church groups, or book review clubs need not be related to vocational or job-grade status. On the job, task forces may be formed from vertical or diagonal slices of the organization to deal with company matters such as safety, trouble shooting, facilities layout, discipline, vacation scheduling, and recreational planning. These groups have membership based on the diversity of knowledge, skills, and interests of the individuals involved and are most effective when they are formed of the free volition of their members. Democracy in the workplace usually avoids groupings based on job grade, gender, age, race, color, religion, and other criteria irrelevant to human aptitude.

When job classification or job-grade level within the organization is the basis for social discrimination and interclass conflict, it usually occurs as a result of restricted and enforced role definitions and officially prescribed symbols of status. However, people free to select their vocational identity and to influence its parameters are less likely to form defensive and aggressive relationships with people who choose to assert their uniqueness. Hence a taxi driver may write poetry, a stone mason may read philosophy, a liberal arts college graduate may paint houses, an electrical engineer may be an electrician, and all may be at peace with themselves and the world, if official authority and judgment do not intrude to force polarizations.

Of course, an organization cannot remedy the problem of a restrictive dress code, for example, by ruling that all people wear informal attire or a common uniform, or insist that all members eat their lunches in a common dining room. This would be just another form of regimentation, not unlike that found in some totalitarian societies, which would violate the freedom of those individuals who, within the constraints of safety and responsibility, may wish to dress formally or eat their lunches from a brown bag or at an off-site location.

However, industrial democracy is supportive of capitalism and the free-enterprise system, but without the reductive use of authority and status symbols. Under industrial democracy, all members of the organization have an opportunity to be creative and productive and are capitalists proportional to their contribution to productivity. The price of this opportunity is, of course, responsibility.

The media through which people achieve industrial democracy may be discussed under three major headings: (1) work systems, (2) interpersonal relationships, and (3) support systems. Work systems center on the work itself that the person was hired to perform. Work itself includes not only the performance of the tasks in the job, but also the planning of one's work and the evaluation of the results. Hence work systems include processes for goal setting and performance evaluation. Work systems also include those aspects of compensation which are related to performance, such as merit pay, performance bonuses, ESOPs (Employee Stock Ownership Plans), profit sharing, and Scanlon-type plans.

Interpersonal relationships refer to the job holder's interaction with anyone in the organization, including those in supervising, peer, and reporting relationships. They include the person's relationships with union leaders, staff personnel, suppliers, and customers, but only to the extent that these relationships relate to job performance. However, they include actual job relationships, official or unofficial and formal or informal, whether or not these appear in an official assignment or job description.

Support systems include all other systems in the organization that are not primarily part of the work systems described above. For example, they might include attitude surveys, lunch rooms and coffee bars, bulletin boards, company newspapers, educational programs, collective bargaining and grievance procedures, air conditioning, and certain types of supplemental benefits. Support systems rarely function autonomously, but share mutually interdependent relationships with work systems and interpersonal relationships.

These three media are, in a complex interactive way, the ingredients for describing the climate of the workplace, ranging from reductive authoritarianism at one extreme to industrial democracy at the other end of the continuum.

THE EUROPEAN INFLUENCE

The state of labor relations in Europe, particularly in Sweden and West Germany, is of continuing interest to representatives of government, labor, and the private sector in North America. Attention has been directed to these two countries for several reasons. In terms of time lost through industrial disputes, Sweden and West Germany have the best records of the major European countries, whereas the United States and Canada are among the poorest performers in this regard. Exhibit 3 shows the number of days lost through industrial strife per 1000 employees in 18 industrial countries during the decade between 1966 and 1975. The chart is somewhat misleading, however, in that the statistics apply only to unionized organizations. In the United States and Canada approximately one-fourth of the labor force is unionized, compared to roughly one-half in West Germany and three-fourths in Sweden. Nonetheless, the chart is significant as a reflection of industrial peace under conditions of collective bargaining.

In addition to its conditions of industrial harmony, West Germany is also studied because of its higher productivity. In terms of productivity per work hour, Sweden has deteriorated 92 percent from 1970 to 1976, Canada 43 percent, the United States 26 percent, and Germany 25 percent. Thus West Germany excels over other major industrial countries in terms of both labor peace and productivity. Highly unionized Sweden, despite its harmonious labor relations, has not been as successful in staying competitive in the world market.

Industrial democracy at the expense of productivity is at best a fleeting and illusory victory. This does not necessarily mean that the Swedish model should be rejected and the West German plan emulated. Each of these

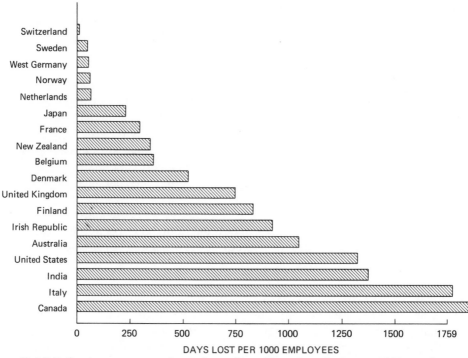

Exhibit 3 Average annual number of working days lost per 1000 employees, 1966-1975, from industrial disputes. ("Canada Has Worst Strike Record," *Industrial Relations and Personnel Developments*, No. 4, January 26, 1977. Reproduced by permission from CCH Canadian Industrial Relations and Personnel Developments, published by and copyright of CCH Canadian Limited, Don Mills, Ontario.)

systems has components which appropriately might be incorporated or rejected in tailoring a system for another culture.

Factors influencing labor relations in West Germany and Sweden are summarized in Appendix A. This information is included not with the implied purpose of encouraging its adoption or rejection in North America or elsewhere, but rather to increase the number of options from which thoughtful managers and union leaders can choose as they forge their own brand of industrial democracy.

Chapter 2

Work Systems

For many people, work is a necessary evil, a requirement for getting the money necessary to buy the things they need. Organizational goals are not their goals; their goals are related to various needs and attractions *away* from the job. These personal goals are often expressed in tangible terms such as a new home, a steady income, a college education, a new automobile, a Caribbean cruise, and a country club membership. For these people, any sense of achievement, growth, responsibility, and recognition is usually experienced away from the job. Their inability to satisfy these higher-order needs on the job cannot be attributed to their inherent or natural characteristics, but rather to the circumstances through which they relate to the organization.

Work systems are characteristically designed on the assumption that the people who operate them are not competent or trustworthy. Systems designers admonish one another to "design the system on the assumption that the operators can't think." And, of course, it becomes a self-fulfilling prophecy when the operators fail to interact intelligently with their "idiot-proof" work systems. The systems designers point scornfully to the operators, saying, "See how stupid they are; they never think!"

However, the operators do think—in retaliatory terms or about things away from the job or how to get away from the job, unfortunately. Hence they make more trips to the water fountain, rest room, first aid center, personnel department, and use up their sick leave. At work they think and talk about their bowling games, camping trips, school board memberships, church activities, do-it-yourself projects, avocational pursuits, job-hopping plans, and miscellaneous fantasies. Or, their thoughts find creative expression in counterproductive activities such as product sabotage, defiance of authority, concerted slowdowns, pilferage, complaints about working conditions, and preoccupation with real or imaginary grievances.

In contrast, many individuals at the upper levels of the organization find their job roles fully as meaningful as their after-hours activities. Their work is intrinsically challenging and rewarding, the most frustrating part of it being their futile attempts to motivate the "ungrateful wretches" at the lower levels of the organization The two-class system, described in Chapter 1, finds expression in the workplace in the relationship between management and labor, as illustrated in Exhibit 4. The social distance and alienation which characterize the gap between management and labor stem from their contrasting roles. Management's role is usually explicitly defined in terms of planning, organizing, leading, and controlling, whereas labor's role is implicitly, or by default, limited to following orders.

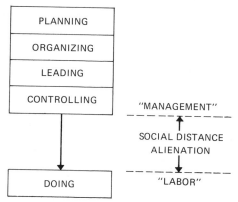

Exhibit 4 The management-labor dichotomy.

EVERY EMPLOYEE A MANAGER

On the assumption that most people are potentially responsible and self-motivated, the mission is to create for the operators the same motivational opportunities experienced by managers. Organizational success depends on making "every employee a manager" by enabling each person to manage a job commensurate with his or her current stage of development, latent capabilities, and personal needs.*

People with meaningful roles in the organization meet their responsibilities in the same spirit that entrepreneurs pursue their organizational goals. In other words, the more a person's job resembles entrepreneurial responsibility, the more likely he or she will feel and act like a manager.

Consider, for example, the self-employed farmer. In terms of the concept illustrated in Exhibit 4, the farmer's work does not create social distance or alienation, as he is representing the two sides of a responsibility which in some organizations is divided by a management-labor gap. However, if the farmer employs helpers, they may or may not experience such a gap, depending on whether they are treated like "self-employed individuals" or as "hired hands."

---

*M. Scott Myers, *Every Employee a Manager,* New York: McGraw-Hill, 1970.

But the farmer too has a meaningful role, as illustrated in Exhibit 5. In the PLAN phase, he plans and organizes his seasonal cycle by developing a marketing strategy, determining acreage requirements, forecasting yields, readying equipment, prescribing pest controls, selecting seed, and crystallizing the planting schedule. The farmer carries out these plans in the DO phase by preparing the soil, planting the seeds, fertilizing, cultivating, applying pesticides, harvesting and marketing crops, and maintaining equipment. The CONTROL, or feedback, phase consists of measuring, evaluating, and correcting, which in this case includes analysis of soil, yields, costs, profits, markets, and the inspection of equipment—all of which provide a basis for modifying next year's plan. The farmer manages this total responsibility within constraints imposed by laws, technology, weather conditions, costs, human resources, schedules, and market conditions.

Exhibit 5 A model for meaningful work.

Members of large organizations, particularly at the lower levels, rarely have the freedom or autonomy experienced by the self-employed entrepreneur. However, the closer to the top of the organization a person works, the more his or her job resembles that of a self-employed individual.

Exhibit 6 shows the PLAN-DO-CONTROL phases of a division head who, as an operating vice-president, is close to the top of the organization. The division head coordinates the planning of R & D, manufacturing and marketing strategies, interdivisional cooperative efforts, organization development, and facilities expansion and has a hand in shaping policy. The DOING aspect of the job involves this person with key customers, in public relations roles, visits to operating sites, the exchange of business information,

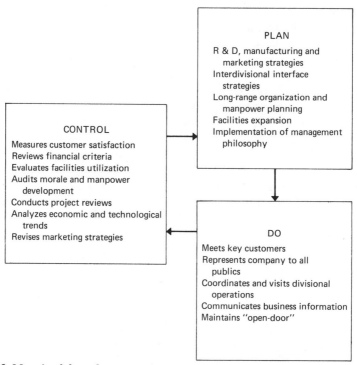

Exhibit 6 Meaningful work—operating vice-president (division manager).

and managing conflict. Control functions include the measurement, evaluation, and correction of factors associated with customer satisfaction, financial performance, facilities utilization, organization development, marketing strategies, and of course with legal constraints. Hence the division director's job offers a balanced combination of plan, do, and control, much like the self-employed individual.

Similarly, Exhibit 7 shows the middle-management job of a manufacturing manager (two levels below the division head) to be quite rich in terms of plan, do, and control. A company is rarely plagued with a poorly motivated manufacturing manager.

Even the foreman's job (first-level supervisor), two levels below the manufacturing manager, may be satisfying in terms of meaningful work concepts. For example, we see in Exhibit 8 that the foreman's job, though narrower in scope than the manufacturing manager's, offers considerable latitude in managing one's own work. Unfortunately, this job, though rich in plan-do-control for the foreman, usually offers little opportunity for the operator to have a meaningful role.

Under this foreman's leadership and within the constraints imposed by company and union policy, the operator (Exhibit 9) lives in a world circumscribed by conformity pressures to follow instruction, work harder, obey

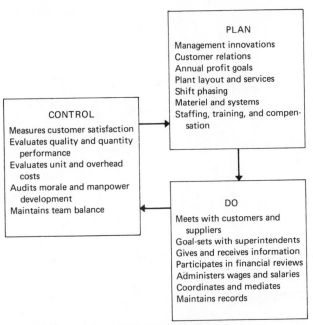

Exhibit 7 Meaningful work—manufacturing manager.

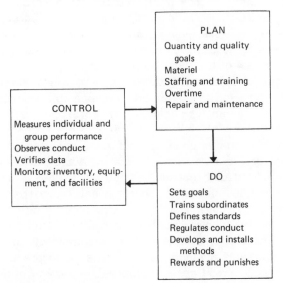

Exhibit 8 Meaningful work—foreman.

rules, get along with people, and be loyal to the supervisor, the company, and the union, most of which tends to quash any satisfaction that work itself might otherwise offer. The operator's role is in a category with equipment, materials, and other nonhuman resources to be manipulated by others in pursuit of their

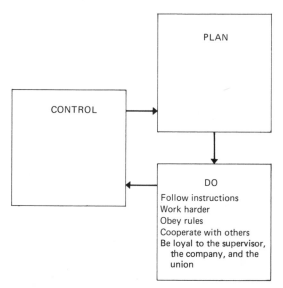

Exhibit 9 Conformity-oriented workers.

organizational goals. Conformity-oriented workers tend to behave like adolescents responding to the punishments and rewards of authoritarian parents, or as primitive tribesmen responding to their tribal chieftain. Persons dissatisfied with organizationally imposed conformity may fight back through the power of the labor union. Union-imposed conformity may result in rebellion in the ranks of the bargaining unit.

The forman's job in some organizations is complicated by the role of the union steward, who also has jurisdictional responsibility for the same people supervised by the foreman. The union leader, in turn, often faces the dilemma of being a subordinate of the foreman on matters of routine job performance, but a peer or even a superior on matters of union business. For instance, it is not uncommon for union leaders to have dealings with top-management people who are not normally accessible to foremen. Thus it is understandable that employees (and their foreman also) often look first to the union steward as the best source of information. Members of a bargaining unit may have, in effect, two supervisors who can put them in conflict situations, particularly if their shop steward and foreman appear to be competing for influence in the organization. However, if union leaders and supervisors are committed in spirit and contract to a relationship of mutual respect and support, these role conflicts are not likely to occur.

Workers culturally conditioned to expect a boss (either company or union) to call the shots may find nothing unusual in the fact that their jobs have little or no planning and control functions. However, the knowledge explosion following World War II, coupled with the gradual displacement of older conformists by the younger enlightened, is making this type of subservient role unacceptable to increasing numbers of people in the workplace. Thus the authority-dominated job shown in Exhibit 9 must be revised to include the planning and control functions illustrated in Exhibits 5-8.

Strategies for restructuring jobs to provide balanced plan-do-control responsibilities compatible with organizational requirements and jobholder capabilities and aspirations may be described in terms of three approaches: (1) jobholder approach, (2) task-force approach, and (3) management approach.

Jobholder Approach

When job incumbents are in methods-improvement programs, such as the Mogensen Work Simplification process described later in this chapter, it may be appropriate to include in this training program the concept of "every employee a manager" and the meaning of plan-do-control. With this orientation, workers can begin analyzing their own jobs in terms of a sequence which begins with the sample items illustrated in Exhibit 10. After completing all items relevant to their kind of work, they can then analyze items in terms of the three basic questions illustrated in Exhibit 11.

In addition, or as an alternative to this approach, job incumbents might be given an opportunity to enrich their jobs by taking appropriate items from their supervisor's jobs. After acquainting them with the plan-do-control concept, show them their supervisor's job, as illustrated in Exhibit 8, and ask

---

PLANNING. Can I as an individual or member of a group—

- Name customers and state delivery dates for products or services?
- State the product quality and quantity commitments?
- Organize work layout, and influence personnel assignments?
- Set goals and standards based on customer needs, and fix priorities?
- State the sources of supplies and equipment and how to obtain them?
- List direct and overhead costs, selling prices, and other profit and loss information?

DOING. Does the job—

- Utilize our talents and require our attention?
- Enable us to see the relationship of our work to other operations?
- Provide access to the information we need to do our work?
- Have a satisfactory work cycle—neither too long nor too short?
- Give us feedback on how well we are doing?
- Give us a sense of accomplishment?

CONTROLLING. Can I as an individual or member of a group—

- State customer quality requirements and reasons for the standards?
- Keep our own performance records?
- Check quality and quantity of work and revise procedures?
- Evaluate and modify work layout on our own initiative?
- Identify and correct unsafe working conditions?
- Obtain information from people outside the group as a means of evaluating performance?

Exhibit 10 Worksheet for analyzing job content.

PLANNING	No	Some-times	Yes
• Does my job allow me to set my own performance goals?	( )	( )	( )
• Is setting my own goals essential to good job performance?	( )	( )	( )
• Do I want more opportunity to set my own performance goals?	( )	( )	( )
DOING			
• Does my job provide variety?	( )	( )	( )
• Is variety in my job essential to good job performance?	( )	( )	( )
• Do I want more variety in my work?	( )	( )	( )
CONTROLLING			
• Does my job allow me to measure my work performance?	( )	( )	( )
• Is opportunity to evaluate my own work essential?	( )	( )	( )
• Do I want more opportunity to measure my own job performance?	( )	( )	( )

Exhibit 11 Job incumbent job-design checklist.

them, "Is there anything in your supervisor's job that you can do, and would like to do?" In a similar way they may be given the opportunity to ask for duties listed in the job descriptions of others such as inspectors and engineers. The enrichment of the operator's job through this process may lead to the partial impoverishment of the jobs from which their new responsibilities were selected.

The incumbents of these newly impoverished jobs may, in turn, go through a similar experience of evaluating their jobs and taking items from jobs in other levels and functions to enrich their own. The net effect of such a process, as it moves continuously upward, is to make jobs more meaningful at all levels. One effect of such a process is not only to enrich the operator's job, but also to change his or her relationship to the supervisor from a conformity-oriented to a goal-oriented relationship, as shown in Exhibit 12.

A comparison of the content of the operator's and supervisor's jobs in Exhibit 12 with the content of their jobs in Exhibits 8 and 9 shows both to be experiencing more meaningful roles and to be utilizing their respective talents more effectively. In other words, each has a job which resembles the model in Exhibit 5, and to the extent that it does, each has a sense of working for self.

The implementation of job enrichment cannot take place without influencing individuals in jobs adjacent to and directly above and below the person whose job is enriched. Therefore, the enrichment of a job cannot be undertaken successfully without the participative involvement of the job-holder and all others (line, staff, and union) who would be affected by the enrichment of the job.

Task-Force Approach

The jobholder approach can be amplified into a task-force effort by having job incumbents, their supervisors, and union leaders work together on the

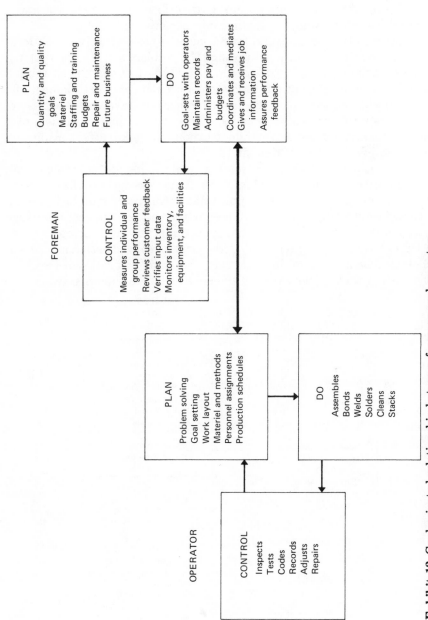

Exhibit 12 Goal-oriented relationship between foreman and operator.

exercises described in Exhibits 10 and 11. The success of this approach, of course, depends on the quality of the relationships of those involved in the process. People in effective work groups, as described in Chapter 4, encounter little difficulty in attaining the relationship depicted in Exhibit 12.

Sometimes the most natural (and hence the most effective) task-force approach to creating a whole job is through the problem-solving, goal-setting procedure involving natural work groups. Here the focus is not on the job itself, but rather on the solution of a customer problem or the attainment of a company goal. For example, the un-self-conscious involvement of store managers, department heads, cashiers, clerk-packers, and customers of a Canadian supermarket resulted in the expansion of a clerk-packer's menial job to the whole job depicted in Exhibit 13.

The consequence of a problem-solving, goal-setting process is more than an opportunity to manage a meaningful job; it also strengthens the organization. For example, the widespread application of this process in the Canadian food chain resulted in a competitive advantage to the organization, which increased job security and promotional opportunity for most members of the work force. Hence to the extent that clerk-packers realized both financial and psychological benefits from their new role, they were in a real sense working for themselves with a joint stake in the success of the supermarket.

Exhibit 13 Clerk-packer as manager.

Management Approach

In some circumstances, it is necessary for managers to design or redesign the jobs of subordinates without the involvement of the persons in those jobs. For instance, in planning a new factory or office in preparation for expansion, long before job incumbents are on the payroll, managers may wish to design facilities, systems, and processes to provide meaningful roles for the people to be hired in the future. A manager in this situation should identify and indoctrinate his or her managerial people as early as possible in order to reprogram their perceptions and to incorporate their ideas in, and evoke their commitment to, meaningful work strategies. Hence a factory manager would involve all managerial people available in an orientation session on the philosophy, goals, and techniques of industrial democracy. As a minimum requirement, this training program should include the plant manager, the personnel director, plant engineer, manufacturing manager, the people who will be in charge of industrial engineering, quality control, EDP, maintenance, and as many as possible of the first- and second-level supervisors. If at this stage the union(s) which will represent members of the bargaining unit(s) is(are) known, union leaders should be included in the job-enrichment planning. Whether or not a union will represent employees in the new facility cannot, of course, be predetermined by upper management, but can be determined only by the employees themselves.

It would be ideal, of course, to include all supervisory people in this advance-planning phase, but in practice new operations usually begin with skeleton staffs and add supervisors as plans are implemented. As new staff are added, they should be selected for their compatibility with the prescribed managerial philosophy and fully oriented before assuming their supervisory roles.

One of the tangible achievements of this skeleton staff is the actual definition of several plan-do-control models based on concepts and procedures reflected in Exhibits 4-11. Before crystallizing managerial jobs, initial effort should be devoted to designing key wage-roll jobs in terms of plan-do-control. Enriching the operators' jobs usually results in the enrichment of supervisors' jobs also, as is shown by comparing the content of the foreman's job in Exhibits 12 and 8.

Thus the plan-do-control model administered in the workplace appeals to a number of human needs, one of which is the sense of autonomy that characterizes the self-employed entrepreneur. Such a person is said to have a joint stake in the success of the organization.

Of course, if all the members of an organization had meaningful roles and in addition owned all the stock in the company, they would in a literal sense be working for themselves. Though such a situation is not a realistic expectation in most places of employment, the essence of entrepreneurial self-employment can be reinforced when stock ownership is a widespread phenomenon in a work force. For instance, a stock-purchase plan or an employee stock-ownership trust which results in company ownership as a broadly shared condition among peers, as described in the next chapter, does much to create the spirit of self-employment.

NATURAL WORK GROUPS

Natural work groups are the primary work systems through which people achieve organizational goals. They are also the most potent media for influencing the quality of interpersonal relationships, which are discussed in Chapter 4.

A natural work group generally consists of a group of peers who work together with their common leader. Such groups might range in size from 2 to 50 members, but more commonly would have 6 to 12 members. Natural work groups can exist at all levels and functions of any type of organization—including, for example, the president and vice-presidents, a superintendent and foremen, a foreman and production operators, a laboratory head and the members of the technical staff, an office manager and clerical staff, an infantry lieutenant and platoon members, a school principal and the teaching staff, a union president and the shop stewards, a telephone crew chief and the members of the repair crew, or a maintenance supervisor and the janitorial group.

The natural work group is potentially a ready-made task force for solving problems and setting goals. Whether it functions as an effective task force pursuing organizational goals or as a counterproductive group is a function of the quality of supervision, as described in Chapter 4.

A supervisor might typically activate the problem-solving, goal-setting process by convening his or her natural work group for the purpose of dealing with specific goal-related problems pertaining to quantity, quality, cost, schedules, or any other situation related to customer or client satisfaction. An actual problem need not exist to call such a meeting; the group may be convened for the purpose of improving a smoothly functioning process. Any process can be improved, and sometimes the anticipatory efforts of the group to reduce costs and improve quality can forestall the encroachment of competitors.

During the first meeting the supervisor should do everything possible to share his or her managerial perspective with the members of the group. People can think and act like managers only to the extent that they see the problem in the same perspective that the upper managers see it. Hence regardless of the organization's charter—be it free enterprise or public sector—the members are made to understand that they are convening to devise better ways of serving their customers or clients and are ultimately accountable to shareholders or taxpayers. Moreover, the supervisor should define the constraints within which they are to pursue the solutions to the problem. Constraints could include, for example, budget limitations, delivery schedules, quality standards, legal restrictions, pricing targets, down-time limits, competitor performance, technical requirements, or any combination of these. All goal setting is done within constraints, and people can be expected to set realistic goals only when they understand these constraints. Constraints cannot always be defined in advance of the problem-solving efforts, but may be introduced during the idea-evaluation stage before goal setting is completed.

Problem-solving, goal-setting meetings are held during regular working hours when possible, but before or after the work shift (with pay) when necessary. The supervisor begins the meeting by candidly stating the problem, providing detailed information (when possible) in terms of history of the project (product or service), duration, delivery schedules, overhead costs, material costs, labor costs, and any relevant constraints, so that all members of the natural work group have a full understanding of the requirements for reaching a profit-making or cost-effective level of attainment. Applying principles and techniques of transactional analysis and conference leadership, the supervisor encourages them to raise questions and discuss the problems informally. When the members of the group appear to have a good understanding of the problem, the supervisor is ready to ask for their suggestions.

Using a flipchart and brainstorming approach, the supervisor records all ideas suggested by the group, with ground rules prohibiting criticism, ridicule, and premature evaluation of the merit of any idea. When further ideas are no longer forthcoming or when time limits are reached, the supervisor begins the evaluation phase.

In reviewing the items, the supervisor avoids statements which evoke defensiveness, such as "Let's go over the items and throw out the half-baked ones" or "Let's review and rank-order the ideas." A far better statement might be, "Let's review the items and not discard any of them, but pick out a few we can all agree with." Such a review and discussion will usually yield only a few recommendations (perhaps less than ten percent of the items on the total list) which the members of the group at that time consider feasible and worthwhile.

Sometimes the most effective role of the supervisor at this stage, when the people are discussing the implementation of ideas, is to encourage this creative process by leaving the room, saying to them something to the effect, "See what you can come up with, and I'll be back in 40 minutes."

It should be noted at this point that asking the group to set a goal is a very essential part of this problem-solving, goal-setting process; unless the group members can relate their performance to an acceptable goal, they will have no basis for evaluating their achievements. Exhibit 14 shows accomplishments of an 11-person team following a joint workshop on problem solving, goal setting. Though goals set by the group were in terms of cost per unit (heavy dotted line), their concerted efforts also resulted in reductions in re-

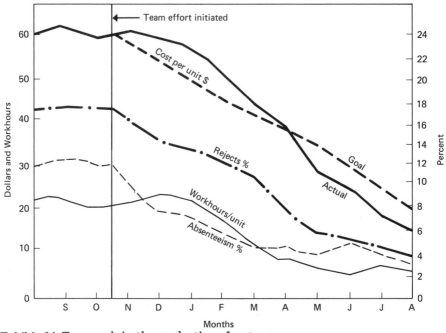

Exhibit 14 Teamwork in the production of water pumps.

jects, absenteeism, and workhours per unit. In terms of their primary goals of reducing the cost per unit, they were behind for six months, but thereafter they surpassed their goals.

A problem-solving, goal-setting meeting usually starts with a natural work group, but may expand later to include others who are not members of the natural work group, whose roles as engineers, inspectors, technicians, buyers, and other staff support personnel can influence the achievement of the mission. These additional resource people are not usually under the organizational jurisdiction of the supervisor who initiates the problem-solving, goal-setting session. In some cases, they are not even members of the organization. The criteria for including a person in the session is his or her stake in the outcome and the ability to contribute to the creative process. Thus a food chain in Canada included supermarket customers, an electronics manufacturing company included vendors, a government service group included welfare recipients, and educators in secondary schools included parents as well as students in their problem-solving, goal-setting sessions.

Outsiders to the natural work groups are not usually invited into the problem-solving, goal-setting session until the members of the natural work group are comfortable in their conference-room role and until they begin to discover their own limitations. If *they* see the need for, and recommend the inclusion of, an industrial engineer, inspector, or customer, these persons can be added without usurping and threatening the basic charter of the group. It is important that these outsiders not be perceived or allowed to act as authority figures in dominating the meeting, but rather as "guests" or "resources."

GUIDELINES FOR PROBLEM-SOLVING, GOAL-SETTING SESSIONS

A natural work group at its best is an effective team for achieving organizational goals. As such, it functions in accordance with the principles described in Chapter 4. As leader of the natural work group, the supervisor plays a key role in expediting the productivity of the group. The summarized guidelines below are provided as a supervisory guide for maximizing work-team effectiveness.

1. **Size of Group** Ideally, a problem-solving group ranges in size from 6 to 12 persons. Smaller groups can be effective, but do not offer the diversity of viewpoints provided by larger groups. Though beginning groups ideally should not exceed 12, as members become comfortable and skillful, additional members may be added. A supervisor with a natural work group of more than 12 members may wish to subdivide it into two or more problem-solving groups to make it possible for all to participate.

2. **Composition of the Group** Every member of a natural work group should participate, even though it may be necessary to subdivide the group to make this possible. As members of the natural work group gradually discover their limitations, resource people from other functions (engineering, quality control, vendors, customers, taxpayers, etc.) may gradually be phased into the work-group meetings. The intervention of nongroup members is done in a style which will not undermine the proprietary responsibility of the natural work group.

3. **When to Hold Sessions** To the extent possible, problem-solving, goal-setting sessions are held during regular work hours and on company time. When work demands do not permit this, meetings are held on a paid overtime basis on a schedule established through advance consultation with members of the group. On-the-job meetings of this type enable people to develop a new self-image—to accept intellectual as well as manual skills as a normal part of their organizational responsibility.

4. **Starting the Meeting** The supervisor starts the meeting with an open, candid, and friendly introduction, presenting a customer requirement or organizational problems to the group and asking for their assistance in solving the problem. The novice conference leader may become trapped in a counter-productive gripe session by telling the group that this is a problem-solving session and asking them to enumerate their problems. Though the group may be productive in enumerating gripes, the focus is usually on parking lots,

eating facilities, air conditioning, coat racks, coffee-breaks, and other maintenance problems. Preoccupation with these dissatisfactions makes it difficult for the group to focus on its purpose for being there, namely, getting a superior product or service to the customers on a cost-effective basis.

5. Defining Constraints All goal setting is done within constraints, and it is important that the supervisor be prepared to enumerate those applying to the group's situation. Constraints may be in the form of time limits, budget limitations, laws, customer commitments, union agreements, company policy, skill limitations, etc. Though all constraints cannot be identified in advance, the rejection of ideas is far more acceptable when resulting from unchangeable constraints than from the arbitrary use of authority. For instance, a recommendation for the purchase of new equipment can be evaluated by the group through a process of sharing the amortization procedure with them.

6. Need for a Goal The creative problem-identification or brainstorming process leads to the compilation of a long list of suggestions and associated ideas. This list has little value until it is translated into one or more goals. When the list is reduced to two or three ideas judged by all concerned to be workable, the supervisor asks the group to estimate, in quantitative terms, the goals it expects to achieve from these changes and a target date for accomplishing them. Goals are to be expressed in tangible terms such as cost reductions in dollars and cents, percent profit improvement, product yield in percentage points, quality standards in terms important to the customer, number of customer complaints per unit of sales, delivery schedules in terms of percent shipments on time, sales efforts in terms of net sales or share of the served available market. Sometimes goal setting is less inhibited if the supervisor leaves the room during the creative process.

7. Importance of Feedback Goals acquire their meaning through feedback. Challenging goals in tangible terms, as illustrated above, are interesting only to the extent that the goal setters receive timely feedback on progress toward the goal. Traditional inspection functions sometimes fail to satisfy this requirement by delaying or distorting the feedback. People in some situations can satisfy their feedback requirements by doing their own inspection, or at least by having instant access to quality-control reports.

8. Techniques of Questioning The appropriate use of questions serves as a stimulant to group participation. Group leaders are aided by their ability to use four types of questions: (1) overhead, (2) directed, (3) reverse, and (4) relay. The overhead question is directed to the total group: "Does anyone have a suggestion?" The directed question is addressed to a specific person: "What do you think, John?" The reverse question is returned to the questionner: "Before I try to answer your question, Bill, have you thought of a possible solution?" The relay question redirects a query to another person: "James, how would you answer Mary's question?"

The experienced conference leader also finds the use of silence to be an effective pump primer. Thus a supervisor who asks an overhead question should be prepared to wait for up to two minutes before interrupting the silence. In practice, such a long wait is not necessary, as few people can tolerate the ambiguity of more than 30 seconds of silence.

9. The Meeting Climate The principles of transactional analysis, as described in Chapter 4, are useful for establishing a climate conducive to constructive spontaneity. Positive strokes nurture freedom of expression, whereas negative strokes inhibit creativity. Adult-Adult, with a sprinkling of Child-Child transactions, foster mutual respect and solidarity, whereas Parent-Child transactions breed not-OK feelings and dependency relationships. The supervisor does not reject an idea through the Parent-Child exercise of official authority, but rather by involving the group in evaluating an idea in terms of specific criteria so that if an idea must be rejected, it is done on the basis of Adult-Adult consensus.

The climate of the meeting is further enhanced by establishing ground rules against ridicule or premature evaluation of suggestions. The supervisor who is sensitive to his or her potential Parent posture as conference leader might democratize the process by bringing additional flip charts into the conference room and asking for volunteers to help in the idea-recording process. Authentic first-name informality is, of course, supportive of a climate of friendliness and mutual respect.

10. Job Security Cost-reduction efforts often lead to savings in personnel costs. However, one of the quickest ways to kill creativity on the job is to lay off people made surplus by their own creativity. Therefore, it is important that people understand that they are assured of an equivalent or better job if displaced from their present assignment. If such an opportunity does not exist, such as during an economic retrenchment, the supervisor may be well advised to postpone group involvement until this economic threat is minimized.

CAN EVERY EMPLOYEE BECOME A MANAGER?

Implicit in the foregoing discussion is the assumption that ideally, every employee should be a manager of his or her job. This is not to say that every person aspires or should aspire to promotional opportunity in supervision or higher-level managerial responsibility. Rather, the term "manager," as used here, refers to the process of managing a job within the limitations established by the individual's capabilities and aspirations.

In a real sense, each person manages his or her own life away from the job. The opportunity for self-management on the job is but an extension of this responsibility in the workplace. And just as the individual in the home and community learns to manage within the legal, moral, financial, and social constraints imposed by society, he or she is potentially capable of performing within the constraints of the workplace.

Some individuals do not manage their own lives successfully in the home and community and seem to require occasional rescue by friends, family, welfare agencies, and counselors. However, the "help" they receive from these protectors is often dispensed in a Parent-Child style that fosters and perpetuates dependency relationships and incompetence. By the same token, these individuals in the organization cannot be expected to be made responsible through the Parent-Child use of permissiveness, coercion, paternalism, persuasion, and manipulation. If ever they are to become responsibly self-reliant, it will be through the influence of Adult-Adult leadership. Indeed, learning to be responsible in the workplace could influence their life-styles away from the job.

But just as some persons choose complex or simple life-styles away from the job, so do individuals differ in their preferred vocational roles on the job. At one extreme, some desire complex and continuously challenging jobs; at the other extreme, others prefer simple, routine jobs. However complex or simple the job, the incumbents have one desire in common: the freedom to choose the job they prefer and to relate to it in a way that is compatible with their own personal values. Hence the concept of "every employee a manager" can have meaning for persons at all levels of talent, though their preferred job-management roles may differ substantially in terms of scope and variety.

Differences among individuals regarding their preferred job roles are more understandable in the light of descriptions of various personality types encountered in the workplace. A personality theory developed by Professor Clare Graves* of Union College helps explain why and how people differ in their choice of vocational roles, as well as their life-styles away from the job.

As humans grow out of infancy and their primary concern with physiological gratification (eating, sleeping, defecation, fondling, warmth, etc.), they develop a "tribalistic" orientation toward life which is reflected in their relationships to their peers and leaders. Their peer relationships tend to be characterized by ritual, common attitudes, solidarity, conformity in dress code, and subservience to "tribal chieftains." During childhood, older siblings, dominant associates, parents, teachers, and police officers are their usual authority figures. If this value orientation carries over into their adult life in the workplace, their supervisor or union leader might become the authority figure they look to for direction, protection, discipline, and affirmation. They often live in a world of magic, witchcraft, and superstition

---

*Clare W. Graves, "Levels of Existence: An Open System Theory of Values," *Journal of Humanistic Psychology* 10, 2 (Fall 1970): 131-135. *See also* M. Scott Myers and Susan S. Myers, "Adapting to the New Work Ethic," *Business Quarterly* (Winter 1973): 48-58.

oriented toward dependency relationships with the "tribal chieftains" in their life. Being a manager of a job at this psychological level means pleasing the supervisor by carrying out prescribed duties or obeying a union leader. Delegation of planning and controlling functions to this person is a valued vote of confidence from the tribal chieftain. Having a whole job is intrinsically satisfying, but more importantly, doing it well earns praise from the boss.

When circumstances lead to greater self-awareness and opportunity for self-expression, tribalistic persons begin asserting themselves as though rebelling against the traditions and authority figures which held them in bondage. The violence of this rebellion is roughly proportional to the amount of talent suppression experienced while in the tribalistic stage. At this rebellious, or egocentric, stage of development, the individual's philosophy of life seems to be, "To heck with the rest of the world—I'm for myself!" On the job, this person's unchanneled hostility and talent lead to "troublemaker" behavior, leaving the individual vulnerable to expulsion from the work force. Though the goal of "every employee a manager" seems unattainable for persons at this stage of development, self-management is an appealing

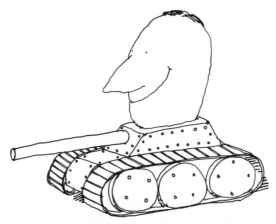

concept to them, and their defiant egocentrism is but an irresponsible expression of their desire to be self-reliant. An appropriate combination of Adult-Adult supervision, peer pressure, and a joint stake in the success of the organization has the potential for giving constructive expression to egocentric talent.

When conditions are conducive to growth, the egocentric's rebellion runs its course and gives way to channeled behavior, usually in support of a cause, philosophy, or religion. This person has low tolerance for those whose values differ from her or his own and is most comfortable with companions with similar conformist viewpoints. However, this person may show devotion to a charismatic leader who supports his or her cause, even to the point of

overlooking limited amounts of unethical behavior. If such a person feels duty-bound and a right to be a manager of his or her job, as officially prescribed by an accepted authority figure, he or she will tackle it with the zeal of a crusader. However, managing a meaningful job may ultimately dissipate the bonds of conformity, in which case the individual may evolve to a new stage of psychological existence.

Ambitious people in the work force often display behavior which may be termed entrepreneurial or manipulative. They are products of the Protestant ethic or Horatio Alger's "rags-to-riches" philosophy and strive to manipulate people and other organizational resources. They pride themselves on their ability to succeed through their own initiative and are inclined to display symbols of their success. Being a manager of his or her own job is this person's natural desire and expectation, and the individual resents supervisory intervention and is intolerant of constraints imposed by policies and procedures.

Though the conformist and entrepreneurial value systems have long characterized the American work force, particularly at the managerial levels, recent years have witnessed rejection of the materialism and commercialism of these value systems. Concern with the quality of life and disdain for traditional status symbols characterize the values of many newcomers to the work force. They tend toward strong affiliation needs—getting along with others seems to be more important than getting ahead in the organization. They wish to be respected by those whom they respect. Though their

informality and sometimes unkempt appearance may be disconcerting to traditional managers, they are capable of productive effort under appropriate supervision and provided they are not involved with what they see as harmful products such as napalm, bombs, or pesticides. Being a manager of their own jobs is an appealing concept to sociocentrics, particularly when they can relate to supervision on a first-name basis and are free to experience solidarity with other members of the work force.

An existential personality type is also encountered with increasing frequency in work forces. He or she tends to ignore protocol, shun status symbols, and resent bureaucratic constraints and the use of authority. This person can accept people whose values differ from his or her own as long as they don't try to impose those values. This person is a goal-oriented individual whose behavior seems to say, "OK, I understand the job to be done; now leave me alone and let me do it in my way." Being his or her own manager is the only acceptable condition of employment, and if deprived of this opportunity, the person is likely to leave the organization or to become preoccupied with personal goals on company time.

In summary, "every employee a manager" is a universally applicable concept, but one that depends on appropriate job conditions for its fullest implementation. Every person has the potential for managing some jobs, but not all jobs. However, every person has the potential for managing certain components of any job or combinations of several jobs. The realization of this potential depends on matching the person's talents and aspirations with the appropriate job, particularly if the employee has an influential role in the matching process. The "job" in this case refers not only to the work itself, but also to style of supervision, procedural constraints, peer relationships, and other climate factors in the workplace.

WORK SIMPLIFICATION

Though the foregoing is a rationale of how every person has the potential for managing job responsibilities, the actual implementation of this concept has been demonstrated for four decades through an innovative training process developed by Allan H. Mogensen, under the deceptive title "Work Simplification."* It is based on the assumption that people don't oppose change; they oppose being changed.

In practice, Work Simplification is job enrichment at its best, which puts the management of change into the hands of job incumbents. Many employees who would like to improve job methods fail to do so simply because they lack the knowledge and analytical skills for formulating improvements. In other cases, where they can and do recommend improvements, they may be frustrated or discouraged by supervisory apathy or hostility. Union leaders sometimes oppose methods improvement if they perceive it as managerial manipulation. If an adversary relationship exists in the organization, the union may be philosophically oriented against any effort interpreted as promanagement. Work Simplification is a natural, un-self-conscious process for endowing job incumbents and their leaders with the skills and attitudes to facilitate self-initiated change.

The following provide the framework for Work Simplification:

1. People do not resist change; they resist being changed.

2. People get satisfaction from their work, especially when they can improve it.

3. Every job is capable of being improved.

4. Every employee has the basic ability to improve his or her job.

5. Improvements are best made by those who perform the job.

6. Most people like to participate in groups.

7. Job-improvement skills are a necessary part of job instruction.

8. The role of the employee is manager of his or her own area of responsibility.

9. The role of the supervisor is one of advisor, consultant, and coordinator.

---

*Work Simplification is being applied in many organizations, but under a variety of titles, including "job management," "operation improvement," "work improvement," "deliberate methods change," "methods change program," "improvement program," and "team improvement program." Whatever the label, the process defined here had its origin in the innovations of Allan H. Mogensen ("Mogy"), whose encounter with displaced creativity in the 1930s led him to develop Work Simplification as a process for enabling job incumbents to share the responsibility for industrial engineering. At the writing of this book, Work Simplification is in its fifth decade of application, still under the guiding influence of Mogy, age 77. The evolution, definition, and application of Work Simplification are described in Auren Uris's "Mogy's Work Simplification Is Working New Miracles," *Factory* (September 1965): 112.

Employees usually learn Work Simplification through standardized company programs implemented by graduates of Mogensen's ten-day winter management workshop at Sea Island, Georgia. Because Work Simplification, as a methods-improvement process, may be perceived as a threat to industrial engineers, many companies have sent them to Mogensen's conferences. Thus not only is their responsibility for methods improvement intact, but it is also broadened to include the encouragement of methods improvement by others. Similarly, union leaders who might otherwise oppose the program are to be involved in its planning and implementation when the concept is being introduced into the organization.

Company training programs are usually taught in two-hour blocks for a total of approximately 20-30 hours. Course content includes principles and techniques of motion-and-time economy, flow-process charting, cost analysis, teamwork, and on-the-job projects for applying newly learned techniques. Projects may be undertaken as an individual or group process and generally follow a five-step pattern:

1. Select a job to improve.
2. Get all the facts.
3. Challenge every detail.
4. Develop the preferred method.
5. Install it—check results.

Work Simplification, broadly applied in all functions and at all levels of the organization, makes "every employee a manager" in terms of the plan-do-control concept described earlier and meets the criteria of an effective system listed in Chapter 6. It is a medium for giving people a psychological and financial stake in the organization, particularly when monetary gains are shared through processes such as profit sharing, Scanlon-type plans, and ESOPs. But most important, Work Simplification is a medium for facilitating the professional growth of people whose initative might otherwise be quashed, and opportunities limited, by traditional supervisory practice, union constraints, and bureaucratic systems.

Chapter 3

Compensation

The compensation individuals receive for their contribution to organizational goals includes both pay and supplemental benefits. The estimated monetary value of supplemental benefits is usually between one-fourth and one-third of the total compensation package.

Unfortunately, the influence of Theory X managers, industrial engineers, social reformers, labor unions, law makers, and consultants has gradually undermined the natural relationship that originally existed between compensation and achievement. In the self-employed craftsmen economy of the Middle Ages, the more creative and productive individuals reaped greater financial rewards. However, in many modern organizations, particularly the larger ones, people are gradually conditioned to relate their pay not to productivity, but rather to the influence of collective bargaining and legislated practice. Not only does this fail to inspire productivity, it actually mitigates against it by sacrificing productivity to featherbedding and the causes of socialistic do-gooders.

The distribution of money often becomes an issue over which company managers and union leaders compete, with little realistic attempt being made to relate compensation to productivity. Thus pay practice is often a manifestation of the jellybean strategy illustrated in Exhibit 15.

Many managers have lost faith in pay as a motivator because so many systems designed to reward high achievers have had some unanticipated side effects which nullified or overshadowed the advantages of merit compensation. For example, the piece-work incentive system, based on engineered standards, has had the dual side effects of quashing the creativity which might otherwise be directed toward methods improvement and activating creativity for thwarting attempts to change methods and tighten standards. In practice, the piece-work incentive—the most commonly accepted merit pay scheme among unionized organizations—leads ultimately to mediocrity. Unions that accept piece-work incentives may do so because labor standards are based on tangible and measurable criteria which can be monitored by union

A tourist named Pavlov,
motoring through a national park,
saw a bear sitting beside the road. **1**

He stopped the car
and rolled down the window,
and the bear came over and peered in. **2**

This was exactly what Pavlov was
told by other tourists might happen,
and he brought along a sack of jellybeans
to feed the bears.

He offered a jellybean,
which the bear devoured with gusto! **3**

But the bear didn't go away. **4**

So Pavlov fed him another,
which the bear ate with apparent enthusiasm. **5**

Delighted with the bear's appreciative response, . . .

But the bear didn't go away. **6**

Exhibit 15 Pavlov and the bear.

Pavlov began feeding him
several jellybeans at a time.   7

But the bear didn't go away.   8

So he continued to feed him jellybeans . . .   9

until the sack was empty.   10
As if to let the bear know he could now withdraw his
head from the window, Pavlov held up the empty sack.

But the bear didn't go away.

He snatched the empty bag, tearing it into pieces,   11
growling malevolently at Pavlov.

Finding no beans in the bag,
he dragged Pavlov from the car . . .

and put Pavlov out of business   12

QUESTION: Is this a bad bear?

Exhibit 15 (cont.)

leaders and job incumbents. However, piece rates ultimately become unmanageable because of the real or imagined inequities which exist among them. When a few workers become satisfied with their labor standards, which are the basis for production bonuses, others, whose tight standards don't permit comparable earnings, are dissatisfied. But when engineers tighten standards of the high earners in the interest of equity, *they* in turn become dissatisfied. They learn to thwart the industrial engineers by opposing methods changes and by limiting productivity. It is not unusual to find workers holding productivity levels to an acceptable level above standard, knowing that the violation of this unwritten code would incur new standards. In one metalworking plant, for example, it is clearly evident each day that most workers have met their "35% over bogie" one or two hours before the end of the shift and are creatively keeping busy in nonproductive activities. Moreover, strong and swift peer pressure is brought to bear on any individual who exceeds the group norm. Hence the piece-work incentive not only fails to increase productivity, but also becomes a major source of dissatisfaction stemming from what job incumbents perceive as unfair management practice. Additionally, some employees are further frustrated by their inability to understand the piece-work incentive system.

Another consequence of the piece-work system is the tendency of people to use it to buy time off with pay. Knowing that surpassing the standard by too high a margin can result in a tightening of standards, employees are tempted to conceal and hoard their overage to cover nonproductive downtime, tardiness, and absenteeism. In a furniture factory, an employee who had been fired for being a troublemaker embarrassed management by turning in hoarded "chits," which forced the company to retain him on the payroll for six additional weeks.

MERIT PAY

Merit pay would seem to be a natural application of motivation principles, and it often is in nonunion organizations. However, unions generally have favored equal pay over merit pay, not because union members do not agree with the concept of merit pay, but rather because they mistrust management's criteria for determining merit. They sometimes accuse management of favoring the company-loyal, antiunion members. If unions doggedly cling to job tenure as the basis of merit, they do so largely because it is tangible, easily explainable to their membership, and less subject to manipulation by management.

Uniform pay tends to satisfy low achievers and dissatisfy high achievers. Merit pay satisfies high achievers and dissatisfies low achievers. Dissatisfied high achievers tend to either leave the organization of find outlets for their talent in counterproductive activities. Low achievers, disappointed through the merit system, have incentive to become high achievers or to leave the organization—either alternative beneficial to the organization, to the individual, and hence to society.

Therefore, the soundest long-range strategy is to develop an equitable merit-pay system that is widely understood and accepted throughout the work force. One of the best ways to make sure that the system is widely understood by those affected by it is to involve union leaders in the development and administration of job evaluation and performance-evaluation methods. A well-informed union leader need not feel defensive about explaining a system he or she understands and believes in.

However, merit pay is not always easily applicable. People whose performance is limited by paced systems and dependence on others have little realistic opportunity to demonstrate meritorious performance. Therefore, implementation of the merit-pay concept must of necessity involve not only the union people, but also industrial engineers and other system designers to provide the degrees of freedom necessary for the high-potential performer.

In practice, the most effective merit-pay system is based on a person-to-person comparative rating system in which individuals are classified into merit categories according to their overall contribution to the success of their organizational unit. Obviously, confidence in such a system depends to a high degree on the climate of trust in the organization in general and confidence in the competence and fairness of supervision in particular. Such a system has greater credibility when more than one level of supervision has a hand in the merit-judgment process. Moreover, people affected by the process must be able to receive an explanation of the factors contributing to the overall rating—which should be keyed as closely as possible to the attainment of tangible goals. Evaluations might include diverse criteria such as quantity, quality, initiative, creativity, dependability, interpersonal relationships, and cost effectiveness, but only if these are clearly related to the attainment of organizational goals. Ideally, members of the work group and their union leaders should have a hand in defining the criteria of job effectiveness.

The success of a merit system also depends on the involvement of the job incumbent in the goal-setting and performance-review processes, as described in Chapter 4. Successfully applied, merit pay represents the same joint stake in the financial success of the organization that is experienced by the self-employed entrepreneur, whose payback is a merit reflection of his or her performance.

No matter how carefully a merit-pay scheme is administered through the joint efforts of management and the union, it has a potentially dissatisfying characteristic—particularly for the enlightened members of the new work ethic. It still depends on judgmental inputs which may appear arbitrary to those affected by it. This characteristic need not disqualify it, provided it is based on describable criteria of merit in particular and takes place in a climate of mutual trust. A climate of trust is developed, of course, by trustworthiness of the company and union leaders on whom people depend for the satisfaction of their psychological and financial needs in the organization.

When the members of an organization have a significant financial and psychological stake in its success, they are not likely to strike against it or to undermine it through other counterproductive activities. However, high pay and supplemental benefits do not necessarily create a motivated and responsible work force. The concept of joint stake is rarely created by paternalism, but rather by conditions which create a team spirit and the opportunity to influence and share in the fate of the team.

Some managers and union leaders scoff at the notion that employees would be willing to share in anything but gain. They say that employees are fair-weather friends who turn against their employer or their union during an economic recession. Such an assumption is valid, of course, when compensation practices reflect a jelly bean mentality. However, people who have a sense of working for themselves are able to respond responsibly to the ups and downs of organizational success.

SHARING PLANS

Compensation schemes that reward individuals in a group for their collective efforts are referred to by Bert Metzger, President of the Profit Sharing Research Foundation, as "total systems incentives."* Under such plans, members of a total group share in benefits derived from cost savings, sales increases, productivity gains, and improved profits.

Profit sharing is one of the more commonly used total system plans, found in approximately one of four companies in American industry. Though profit-sharing plans differ significantly in administrative details and can work in either union or nonunion situations, they have in common the sharing of a portion of the company profits with members of the work force. The most effective profit sharing plans have the following characteristics:

1. They apply to all members of the work force, both hourly paid and salaried.

2. All members share equitably in the distribution of the shared pool, in most cases as a percent of the base pay, but occasionally, in equal amounts. In cases where other compensation plans remunerate people in higher job grades adequately for their greater accountability, more mileage might be obtained by distributing the fund in equal shares to all members of the organization. However, care must be exercised to make sure that total compensation packages proportionately reflect contribution to organizational performance.

3. The amount allocated for profit sharing is enough to make it seem worthwhile to the members and is realistically related to profits. Though

---

*Bert L. Metzger, "Profit Sharing—One of the New Breed of Total Systems Incentives," *Atlanta Economic Review* (May-June 1974): 60-62.

small or zero profit sharing can be understandable and acceptable in lean years, higher payout is expected when profits are up. Consistently small payouts, particularly when members don't understand the formula, are often perceived as tokenism or managerial manipulation.

4. Members of the organization understand the formula through which the profit-sharing fund is determined. Though the amount set aside for distribution to members is typically discretionary with top management (along with allocations for stock dividends, facilities maintenance and expansion, research, and engineering, etc.), it is important that the members who wish to know can understand the logic which creates the profit-sharing fund and that union leaders, in particular, understand and accept the formula and be prepared, if necessary, to explain it to their members. Some organizations publish formulas to enable members to make current estimates of future profit-sharing payouts.

5. Feedback on benefits is frequent and timely. Plans that give members prompt quarterly or monthly status reports are more effective than those that present only a year-end annual report, particularly if the annual report is delayed a few months. Frequent and current reporting keeps people "in on the know" and enables them to respond responsibly to business fluctuations.

6. Members have a hand in managing their individual profit-sharing accounts. For example, options might include annual or semiannual decisions on how individual accounts should be invested and how much of the account is to be received in cash and how much is to be deferred. A plan that permits monthly or quarterly payout of one-half the estimated ultimate benefit provides tangible feedback and still provides an annual contribution to the deferred account for discretionary investing.

7. Participants should be protected against bureaucratic inflexibilities which defeat the purpose and spirit of the plan. For example, safeguards should be provided against the mandatory payout of a depressed profit-sharing account resulting from retirement during a business recession.

8. Members are prepared financially and psychologically to take the lean periods in stride. In plans providing for periodic cash payouts, for example, members of the plan could reach agreement on a formula for both profit sharing and "loss sharing." They might, for example, agree to hold 15 percent of the quarterly payout in escrow as a hedge against lean periods. Obviously, the more that people understand about corporate finance in general and their specific plan in particular, the more likely they are to respond maturely to fluctuations in shared benefits.

9. Members have an opportunity to apply their talents and efforts in tangible ways to influence company profitability. People who are active in improving methods, participating in problem solving, goal setting,

cost reduction, quality improvement, productivity acceleration, and preventive maintenance feel a greater proprietary interest in their profit-sharing plan than do employees whose roles are circumscribed by company procedures, union by-laws, and routinized systems.

American Velvet Company*

American Velvet, a major velvet producer located in New England, owes much of its success to its profit-sharing plan, which was installed in 1940 after a 16-month strike. The late Clarence Wimpfheimer, owner of the company, was shocked by the strike, and soon thereafter he instituted a profit-sharing program aimed at ending the bitterness which developed during the long conflict.

Profits have been made each year since 1939, and thus bonuses (or "earnings") have been paid regularly. The company has experienced no strike or unauthorized walkout, and no grievance has gone to arbitration. Company officials point to the "tight" way the mill is run and the high employee level of effort as the reasons that American Velvet has not followed its competitors South, where textile wage rates are lower and unionization almost nonexistent. Management contends that this situation is the result of cooperative feelings stemming from profit sharing—that blue-collar workers are aware that benefits will not be received if the company is not profitable. Southern competitive pressures also exist, and employees realize that if the firm is not profitable, it may be forced to move South and that their jobs will be lost.

Innovations are usually initiated by management, but only after checking them out with union officials whose support is needed. This seems to be the key to the relationship, because once the union is made aware of the competitive advantage of a new policy, it communicates this change to the work force and helps the company install the changes.

The plan distributes 27 percent of profit before taxes to eligible employees—one-third in cash, one-third deferred, and the remaining third to be deferred or paid in cash at the option of the individual.

Jacques D. Wimpfheimer, President of American Velvet Company, offers this viewpoint:

> Profit sharing offers flexibility on the wage side that is most desirable. . . . It creates and rewards increased productivity and builds understanding and cooperation between labor and management.

> The American Velvet Company has, since its installation of profit sharing in 1940, been in the unique position of never having a losing year. Profit sharing has ranged from a low of five per cent to a high of thirty-nine per cent (of wages).

---

*Excerpted from Herbert R. Northrup and Harvey A. Young, "The Causes of Industrial Peace Revisited," *Industrial and Labor Relations Review* 22 (October 1968): 31-47.

Best of all, we have not had a single strike nor have we gone to arbitration to solve a single one of our problems.

Both labor (Textile Workers Union of America) and management take the attitude that the company is a living organism off which we all live, and the stronger it is, the better off we all are.

Clarence Pollard, when Secretary-Treasurer of Local 110, Textile Workers Union of America, stated:

Under profit sharing, I feel like a holder of common stock. If the company prospers I'll get a good dividend, knowing that to make a company prosper the workers have to do their share. I feel that under profit sharing our union is much stronger than a union without a profit sharing plan. We understand not only our own problems, but the company's also. We have a better concept of economics knowing that productive efficiency can be increased whenever labor and management sincerely want to work together.

Joseph Sposato, former President of Local 110, said:

It would be very difficult indeed to establish a profit sharing plan and expect it to motivate your employees into a higher rate of productivity and sound labor-management relations without first discussing the entire plan with the union and your employees; allowing them the opportunity of expressing their views. To be effective it must be a mutually acceptable product.

Our union suggested in 1940 that a program to educate the employees on profit sharing and simple economics be undertaken as soon as possible. To start this program, meetings were held weekly. Our employer would invite about forty employees up to his office on company time. We held discussions, and blackboards were used for illustration. After every employee had attended these "classes," we then held "classes" once a month with a good visiting speaker.

An analysis of a successful marriage between a successful enterprise and a union will bear out the fact that it is not accomplished by one party going its own way alone, but because both parties took time to communicate and cooperate in the planning that would solve their mutual problems. Our everyday communications is done on an informal basis. We use our various committees as avenues of communication.

Because we learned to communicate our feelings, point to our objective, and care about each other's problems, we have gradually become educated to the complexities of running a business to make a profit. Management realizes that it can depend upon a great share of cooperation from us, its employees, if we are treated like human beings instead of machines. This is achieved only by having us fully participate in the work of the company.

Compensation **3**

Union Attitudes Toward Profit Sharing*

Historically, American unions have been hostile or indifferent to profit sharing. In the unions' early days, bread-and-butter issues such as wages, working conditions, and union security were the chief goals. Labor leaders were suspicious of profit sharing, feeling that management used it to avoid unionization or paying decent wages, or both. However, union attitudes, at least in some circles, have changed over the years.

There is no universal union attitude toward profit sharing. Although many large companies (with or without unions) engage in profit sharing, most very large unionized companies do not. Some union leaders still oppose profit sharing because they believe it intrinsically conflicts with the traditional adversary approach to labor-management relations. Other union leaders believe that their members' jobs will be secure (not exported overseas) only if labor collaborates with mangement in increasing productivity and shares in the gains on some flexible basis. In this way, employees can get their full equity without causing inflationary pressures which undermine their own job security. The difference in attitude in part reflects the experience of various union people with different profit-sharing programs.

The late Walter P. Reuther, President of the United Auto Workers, became aware of the limitations of traditional collective bargaining in the years immediately preceding his death:

> The stress in collective bargaining . . . stems in large part from the fact that neither management nor labor really knows what the true equity of the workers will be over the full term of the contract. . . .† If a contract is negotiated at the peak of prosperity, the workers may be able to obtain gains that will impose heavy costs on the firm if the market for its products slackens. Conversely, a contract negotiated at the trough of a recession may saddle the workers for three years with wage and fringe benefit gains far smaller than those the company will actually be able to afford. . . .Profit sharing would resolve the conflict between management apprehensions and worker expectations on the basis of solid economic facts as they materialize, rather than on the basis of speculation as to what the future might hold. . . .‡

Profit Sharing in Large Companies

Listed on p. 51 are the 36 largest (1973) industrial, retailing, and banking companies with profit-sharing plans.

---

*Excerpted from Bert Metzger, "Profit Sharing: Capitalism's Reply to Marx," *Business and Society Review* (Autumn 1974): 37-45.

†UAW statement to General Motors, July 28, 1967.

‡Walter Reuther's statement on the President's Economic Report, presented to the Joint Economic Committee, February 20, 1967.

Industrial companies
American Brands
Bell & Howell
Burlington Industries
Deluxe Check
Eastman Kodak
Halliburton
Kellogg
McGraw-Edison
Motorola
Polaroid
Prentice-Hall
Procter & Gamble
Schlumberger
Signode Corporation
Sohio
Standard/California
Tektronix, Inc.
Texas Instruments
Time, Inc.
Union Oil
Whirlpool
Xerox
Zenith Radio

Retailing companies
Carter Hawley
Federated Department Stores
J. C. Penney
Jewel Companies
Lowe's Companies
Safeway Stores
Sears, Roebuck
Southland Corporation
Walgreen
Winn-Dixie

Commercial banking companies
BankAmerica
Chase Manhattan
Manufacturers Hanover Trust

Unions in profit-sharing companies (principal unions with members covered by profit-sharing plans)
American Federation of Grain Millers
Brewery Workers
Independent Radionic Workers
Int. Assoc. of Machinists
Int. Brotherhood of Electrical Workers
Int. Brotherhood of Teamsters
Int. Union of Electrical, Radio, and Machine Workers
Int. Union of Petroleum Workers
Ivorydale and St. Bernard Employees' Representation Association
Meat Cutters
Newspaper Guild of New York
Oil, Chemical, and Atomic Workers
Restaurant Employees
Retail Clerks Int. Assoc.
Retail, Wholesale, & Dept. Store
Tobacco Workers Int.
United Steel Workers
Xerographic Division, Amalgamated Clothing Workers of America

Compensation **3**

KELSO'S ESOP

An innovative supplement to traditional compensation systems is being introduced into increasing numbers of American organizations under the label of ESOP (Employee Stock Ownership Plan). Developed by lawyer-economist Louis O. Kelso over the last two decades, the plan is finding widespread acceptance by conservatives and liberals alike. The ESOP offers an opportunity to engender an entrepreneurial spirit in society by evoking a proprietary interest in the success of the organizations that offer them.

As noted earlier, self-employed people are highly motivated and by definition are working under a compensation plan which inspires commitment, productivity, and innovation. However, most workers in American industry don't work for themselves; they work for the shareholders, who own all or most of the stock of the companies that employ them. Because most of these absentee owners are not on the payroll of the companies whose shares they own, they have little opportunity to influence productivity within these organizations. Employees who work for governmental agencies are no better off, as relatively few American taxpayers are inspired to higher productivity simply because a small slice of their taxes supports the organization that employs them. Thus except for the small percentage of people who are actually self-employed or have a significant ownership in their employing organizations, American workers are working for someone else. As has already been discussed, however, people are motivated by their own goals, not the goals of others.

The ESOP is described diagrammatically in the solid lines in Exhibit 16. Kelso has described this plan and its ramifications in several books and articles, and the concept has been evaluated in numerous trade journals and management periodicals.*

ESOP combines employee-benefits plans with corporate financing to the mutal benefit of the corporation and its members. A company sells stock to the ESOP trust for the purpose of raising operating capital and/or inspiring productivity or creating a viable retirement plan. The ESOP trust borrows money to buy the stock and may pledge stock and/or use company guarantee as security. Within specified limits, employer contributions to qualified ESOPs are tax deductible, and bank debts (both principal and interest) are repaid with pretax earnings.

Employees receive ownership in company stock proportional to their gross income. Hence both income level and company tenure influence the amount of a second income they collect when they leave the organization.

---

*Louis O. Kelso and Mortimer J. Adler, *The Capitalist Manifesto*, New York: Random House, 1958; Louis O. Kelso and Patricia Hetter, *Two-Factor Theory: The Economics of Reality*, New York: Random House, 1967; W. Robert Reum and Sherry Milliken Reum, "Employee Stock Ownership Plans: Pluses and Minuses," *Harvard Business Review* (July-August 1976): 133-143; Charles G. Burke, "There's More to ESOP than Meets the Eye," *Fortune* (March 1976): 128.

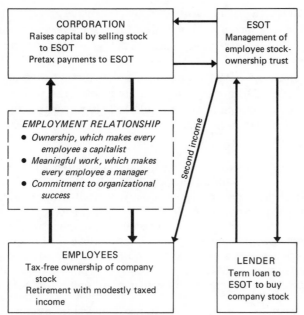

Exhibit 16 Employee stock-ownership plan.

Individuals pay no tax on their stock ownership until they leave the organization, at which time it is taxed at a lower retirement income rate as permitted by the Internal Revenue Code.

Critics of the plan have made their assessments almost exclusively on the basis of the ESOP as a process for raising money and/or a method of financing a retirement plan—that is, the portion of ESOP portrayed in Exhibit 16 in solid lines. This viewpoint does not give adequate recognition to the plan's potential for enchancing the motivation of the work force—as described in italics within the dotted lines in Exhibit 16.

The employment relationship portrayed in this diagram underscores the importance of synergizing meaningful work concepts, described in Chapter 2, with capital ownership to obtain proprietary commitment to organizational goals. From the perspective of enlightened workers, the plan creates economic justice with a motive for high achievement. The ESOP represents one of the rare situations in which people can receive a free benefit without its being perceived as a jellybean. The reason, of course, is that the value of the stock is, or becomes, a function of employee productivity. Therefore, the payout from ESOP is an earned reward rather than a manifestation of paternalism.

The compulsion to work, once created by the Protestant ethic, is now being replaced by a joint-stake reason to work. People who manage challenging jobs and receive financial feedback proportional to their accomplishments can experience dignity and self-reliance.

Unlike socialism, which tends to quash incentive and level incomes, the ESOP reinforces initiative by rewarding high achievers. For instance, the higher merit pay and discretionary bonuses of higher achievers are reflected in their greater ownership in ESOP. Increased productivity renders an organization more competitive and profitable—further increasing the cash value of the ESOP. Moreover, the joint financial stake which people share with the company and one another tends to bring peer pressure to bear on counterproductive members. The philosopher-educator Mortimer J. Adler says of the ESOP:

> According to Mr. Kelso's theory, capitalism perfected in the line of its own principles, and without any admixture of socialism, can create the economically free and classless society which will support political democracy and which, above all, will help us to preserve the institutions of a free society. In what we have become accustomed to call "the world-wide struggle for men's minds," this conception of capitalism offers the only real alternative to communism, for our partly socialized capitalism is an unstable mixture of conflicting principles, a halfway house from which we must go forward in one direction or the other.*

Second incomes derived from stock ownership render retirees less dependent on social security and in some cases might even displace it. Unlike social security, which punishes the fiscally responsible by depriving them of the annuity to which they contributed, ESOP also rewards retirees who continue to be high achievers.

Perhaps one of the greatest consequences of the ESOP is its potential for redirecting the human energy now being dissipated in adversary relationships. As long as management is comprised of the "haves" and labor of the "have-nots," win-lose strategies will be perpetuated between company and union over bigger shares of a diminishing pie. Under ESOP, in which all employees are part owners, union leaders on the board of ESOP represent employees as shareholders rather than as adversaries. People working for themselves strive to increase the size of the pie and do not strike against themselves or engage in other counterproductive measures.

The full fruition of ESOP in the United States, as envisioned by Kelso, is dependent on the enactment of pending legislation now being favorably considered. However, with facilitative legislation already enacted, ESOP has much to offer to support the cause of social and economic justice and to preserve capitalism and the free-enterprise system. Countries that at present do not offer financial incentive for the ESOP may capitalize on the potential it offers simply by enacting facilitative legislation.

---

*Louis O. Kelso and Mortimer J. Adler, *The Capitalist Manifesto,* New York: Random House, 1958, p. xvi. Reprinted by permission.

A report in *Time* describes the circumstances leading to the establishment of an ESOP in South Bend Lathe Company and the reaction of the employees to the plan:

More worker-owners

WELCOME TO SOUTH BEND LATHE, AMERICA'S LARGEST 100 PERCENT EMPLOYEE OWNED COMPANY. So reads the proud sign in front of a sprawling red brick factory in South Bend, Ind. Little more than a year ago, the 70-year-old machine-tool maker faced liquidation because its performance was not up to the expectations of its owners, Amsted Industries, Inc., a Chicago-based conglomerate. But South Bend was a solid company with good years ahead of it, thought some of its top executives. They went shopping for a way to buy the company and pump in enough working capital to keep it going until times got better. Today South Bend is doing well and is totally independent, with most of its stock already deposited in a trust in which each of the company's 440 employees share, according to salary and seniority. SBL's turnaround probably owes much to the U.S. economic recovery, which has sharply driven up orders for machine-tool producers. But the company might not exist at all were it not for a financial device called ESOP, or Employee Stock Ownership Plan.

ESOP is no fable. The device is becoming increasingly popular as a way for companies to raise needed capital and give employees a stake in the business. As in the case of South Bend Lathe, an ESOP can help a basically sound business to keep going when it would otherwise be sold off or closed down. But its use is not limited to such last-chance situations. According to the Internal Revenue Service, more than 250 firms now operate some form of ESOP program, including such corporate successes as Hallmark Cards of Kansas City, Mo., Gamble-Skogmo, a Minneapolis-based retailer with 18,000 employees; E-Systems, Inc., a Dallas defense contractor; and Houston's Zapata Corp.

Tax Break. The main attraction is that an ESOP gives a company a huge tax break. The mechanism: an employee trust is set up, borrows money and uses it to buy newly issued stock from the company. Then the company makes contributions to the trust that are used to repay the loan; they are contributions to an employee benefit plan and are tax deductible. Had the company borrowed the money directly, it would be able to deduct only the interest as a business expense. When the money goes through ESOP, the company can in effect deduct principal repayments too, thus cutting borrowing costs by as much as half.

Even that is not all. In recent years Russell B. Long, the conservative but populist chairman of the Senate Finance Committee, has become an evangelical disciple of Louis O. Kelso, a San Francisco attorney who has long championed various forms of "worker capitalism." In 1974 and 1975, Long pushed through legislation increasing the 10% investment-tax credit that a company gets for purchases of new equipment to 11%—provided that the extra 1% is used to pay for company stock

55

distributed to employees through an ESOP. This year Long pushed further; that 1% special credit (which is directly subtracted from the tax a company owes) has increased to 1-1/2% in the tax-reform bill that Congress passed last month (*Time*, Sept. 20). The extra half-point, however, is available only if employees dig into their own pockets and invest a matching amount in the company's stock. American Telephone and Telegraph Co., which has more than 770,000 employees, is now considering setting up a limited ESOP. Such a plan could have saved Ma Bell $80 million in 1975 taxes alone.

Critics of the tax breaks argue that they amount to a gift from the Government that will mainly benefit high-salaried workers in such capital-intensive industries as oil drilling and machine tools. They are the industries that use the investment-tax credit most heavily, and their capital needs make them especially likely to grab at what amounts to a chance to borrow at low cost.

But the ESOP idea has strong support from Congress's Joint Economic Committee, and the Economic Development Administration of the Department of Commerce is actually requiring that some companies to which it gives loans establish ESOPs.

The most powerful defense of ESOP comes from Long, who waxes as fervent on the subject as Kelso. The Louisiana Democrat contends that the idea will spur managers to invest more of the $3 trillion to $5 trillion that economists say will be needed over the next decade to modernize U.S. industry—besides the philosophical benefits to capitalism of having workers become owners. ESOP, says Long in a burst of lyricism, "is better than Geritol. It will increase productivity, improve labor relations, promote economic justice. It will save this economic system."

Measuring up. Labor leaders have been ambivalent about ESOP, but at South Bend Lathe, United Steelworkers Union members are enthusiastic, and two local representatives sit on the company's board of directors. Union Organizer June Molnar, 26, a tool and cutting grinder, reports that workers check out new recruits to be sure they measure up. Slacking off is not tolerated, says Molnar, who expects to get about $2,000 deposited in her ESOP account this year: "It's 'Hey, you've got your hand in my pocket if you don't do your job.'" Molnar's boss, SBL President Richard Boulis, 53, is just as ebullient. Contemplating a 20% rise in productivity in the past year and close to 10% more pretax profits during the first year of independent operation, he exults, "Worker-owned companies are the way to go."*

In summary, the ESOP concept has potential for solving or ameliorating a number of interdependent problems:

1. Enlightened members of American work forces are reacting negatively to traditional wage systems in general and to paternalism in

---

*"More Worker-Owners," *Time*, October 4, 1976, p. 80. Reprinted by permission from *Time*, The Weekly Newsmagazine; Copyright Time Inc. 1976.

particular. Their broader perspective enables them to see the merits of an ESOP, which gives them a joint financial stake in the success of the organization.

2. The compulsion to work, based on the Protestant ethic, is giving way to the quest for meaningful work. For many, being on relief is no less demeaning than being a highly paid automaton. The ESOP fosters a new work ethic, but on a rational foundation of productivity and responsibility.

3. Per capita productivity is gradually declining across the nation, resulting in inflation, competitive disadvantage in the world market, and balance-of-trade deficits. Though federal treasury receipts are temporarily reduced, less tax revenue is needed to finance relief programs. Actually the accelerated cash flow activated by increased discretionary income of retirees has potential for maintaining tax revenues. Hence the reward system of ESOP increases productivity and thus benefits the nation, as well as organizations and their members.

4. Leaders in government and business are increasingly concerned that recent trends can lead America into socialism and the debilitating bureaucracy now being experienced in Great Britain. Managers recognize the need to improve the economic status of workers, but are deathly afraid of giving the company away. ESOP at once improves worker status and bolsters the free-enterprise system. Though originally designed for profit-making organizations, the ESOP can be adapted to the public sector to apply, for example, to postal services, universities, and municipal administration.

5. The social security retirement system is near bankruptcy, and the income needs and expectations of retirees are accelerating at a faster rate than contemporary taxpayers can support them. The second income created by an ESOP constitutes a supplement which can reduce tax burdens and increase retirement incomes.

6. Unions are making inroads into the public sector and what were heretofore recognized as the ranks of management—unionism is becoming less of a white-collar/blue-collar dichotomy. Traditional unionism, basing its existence on adversary relationships, tends to convert people into opponents squabbling over greater shares of a shrinking pie. ESOP has the potential for converting the win-lose mentality of labor relations into collaborative win-win strategies through which people increase the size of the pie.

Chapter 4

Interpersonal Relationships

People relate to one another in the workplace through the language of words, behavior, and systems. The language of words refers to spoken or written words that people hear or read. The language of behavior pertains to nonverbal communications such as facial expressions, gestures, supervisory styles, social interactions, recreational groupings, task-force endeavors, and freedom of action. The language of systems alludes to procedural media such as attitude surveys, job posting, grievance procedures, public address systems, performance reviews, work standards, and other processes utilizing standardized forms and equipment.

These three types of communication media obviously are not mutually exclusive. For instance, performance reviews usually involve all three— words, behavior, and systems. Information is conveyed via written and spoken words to the person being evaluated. Vivid messages are also conveyed by the supervisor's mannerisms, facial expressions, and tone of voice. The standard forms and procedures represent a system which circumscribes the communication process.

Behavior and systems may be though of as the language of action and are generally considered to be more influential than the language of words. It is sometimes said that when the language of action differs from the language of words, the language of action is the only one "heard." For example, with the language of words a management spokesperson may say, "People are our most important assets," but with the language of behavior may contradict these words by frowning and failing to listen. And with the language of systems, management may reinforce this contradiction through the inappropriate use of time clocks, signal bells, work standards, and status symbols.

How we communicate with people has become increasingly important as people have become more enlightened. Enlightened people do not like to be talked down to, as some parents talk down to children. People respond better if they are addressed as adults. However, unenlightened people who are more accustomed to dependency relationships may expect to hear the voice of authority, accept it as normal, and even welcome it as an expression of parental concern.

TRANSACTIONS

The late Eric Berne* pointed out that each personality has three components which for the purpose of explanation to nonpsychologists, he labeled Parent, Adult, and Child. Each person has these three dimensions within his or her personality, ready to respond to appropriate cues. The Parent is talking when a supervisor says, "I warn you not to be late again"; the Adult says, "We needed you at eight o'clock this morning"; and the Child says, "Please don't come in late; you'll get us both in trouble."

When the Parent part of the personality is active, it may be expressed in one of two ways—critical or protective. The Critical Parent may be judgmental, fault-finding, self-righteous, hostile, tough, or dogmatic. The Protective Parent may be sympathetic, kind, helpful, nurturing, indulgent, and affectionate.

The Adult component of the personality is rational, logical, factual, and unemotional. It is the data processor within us and sometimes is referred to as our computer.

The Child component of the personality may be expressed in one of two ways—as a Natural Child or as an Adapted Child. The Natural Child is creative, intuitive, fun-loving, charming, and optimistic, or self-indulgent, selfish, domineering, and manipulative. The Adapted Child tends to be compliant, courteous, depressed, whining, withdrawing, and vindictive.

It should be noted that reference to Parent, Adult, and Child is not related to chronological age. People of all ages have these three components in their personalities. Very young as well as older people may have what may be called strong Parent tapes—that is, their minds have recordings on them, like cassette tapes, imprinted by their parents or other authority figures. Typical Parent tapes are:

If at first you don't succeed, try, try again.

Eat all the food on your plate.

Boys don't cry.

Girls don't get dirty.

Never tell a lie.

By the same token, older people may have strong Child components, and hence we see 65-year-olds enjoying a party, going to a picnic, watching television, eating ice cream, pouting about a disappointment, or withdrawing within themselves.

---

*Eric Berne, *Transactional Analysis in Psychotherapy*, New York: Grove Press, 1961.

People of all ages, then, have active Parent, Child, and Adult personality components. The Adult component enables us to take an objective look at ourselves, to understand how our Parent and Child are influencing our behavior, and to help us decide whether or not to permit this to happen. For example, the obese person who has been served a piece of coconut cream pie hears three voices:

Parent: "You shouldn't eat it, fatty!"

Child: "I want it! After all, life is to be enjoyed."

Adult: "I'd enjoy it for five minutes and carry it around for five weeks."

The Child may win out, the Parent arouses guilt feelings, but the Adult analyzes what happened and, if the desire for pie is strong enough, may work out a calorie budget to allow for pie in the diet.

In the workplace, a person's perceptions and expectations are influenced by the component that may be dominant. Consider, for example, the immediate reaction of the individual who is told, "Hey, Joe, the boss wants to see you in his office—right now!" Depending on which component of his personality is activated at that time, Joe might experience any of the following feelings:

Critical Parent: "Why can't he leave me alone when I'm busy?"

Protective Parent: "Don't worry Joe—everything will be OK."

Adult: "I wonder what he wants to see me about."

Natural Child: "Wow, maybe I'm getting a promotion!"

Adapted Child: "Oh, no—I hope I didn't do anything wrong."

In his supervisor's office, Joe may receive either positive or negative strokes. Speaking from his Adult, the supervisor might give him a positive stroke: "Thanks for coming in, Joe, I would like your advice. The superintendent wants to know when we could get the new compressor installed. What shall I tell him?" Or, speaking from his Parent, the supervisor could give Joe negative strokes on the same subject: "Where in the devil were you, Joe? I promised the super we'd have the new compressor installed by tomorrow noon. Drop whatever you're doing and get on it, or it's your neck and mine. Now don't tell me your problems; I don't want to hear from you till the job is done."

The use of positive strokes is more likely to evoke an Adult-Adult discussion between Joe and his supervisor, resulting in mutual respect and self-confidence. The negative strokes clearly represent a Parent-Child encounter, which forces Joe's Adapted Child to say, "Yes, sir," resulting in lingering resentment and anxiety.

A positive stroke in its simplest form may be a smile or a friendly gesture—a warm sign of acceptance. A negative stroke may be a frown, a sneer, or a criticism—a putdown. In the work environment, asking for suggestions and listening to them are positive strokes. Not listening to ideas or giving "idiot-proof" job instructions are negative strokes. Not all positive strokes have to be good news. In the discussion of performance review later in this chapter, it is shown that adverse information, handled as feedback, represents a display of confidence and respect which makes it a positive stroke.

As a consequence of continuous use of positive or negative strokes, people tend to develop a rather permanent set of attitudes toward themselves, others, and life in general. This attitudinal life position is sometimes referred to as degree of "OKness." A person who is consistently treated as an adult and given many positive strokes tends to develop feelings of OKness about self and others. This person's basic position is "I'm OK, you're OK"; the world is a pretty good place, and it's fun to be alive. But the person who is given many positive strokes from permissively protective authority figures may develop a spoiled-brat syndrome of "I'm OK, you're not OK." Individuals who have received a lifetime of negative strokes may develop the position "I'm not OK, you're OK" or "I'm not OK, you're not OK." This is particularly true of persons whose initiative has been continuously quashed or who have been unfairly and inescapably disadvantaged in competitive pursuits.

Many individuals appear to carry through life a characteristic position of OKness which predictably manifests itself in most circumstances. For most people, however, feelings of OKness are situational. For example, an employee in the workplace may feel "I'm OK, you're not OK," in church may feel "I'm not OK, you're OK," but at home feel "I'm OK, you're OK."

People are sometimes polarized into positions through their group identity. In a company of stressful labor relations, management people seem to assume a uniform position toward the union members of "We're OK, they're not OK." Union members in turn assume the position "We're OK, but management is not OK." As long as these basic group postures exist, it is not realistic to expect collaboration between the two parties.

Strokes and life positions are interdependent. When our Critical Parent or defiant Child causes us to dispense negative strokes, we may evoke an "I'm not OK" or "You're not OK" attitude from the recipients. When our Adult or Natural Child applies positive strokes, we usually evoke "You're OK" responses. However, people in the "We're OK, you're not OK" position find it unnatural and difficult to dispense positive strokes to the "enemy," and so the mutually self-defeating win-lose cycle is perpetuated. The interruption of this win-lose cycle can be constructively activated only by unusual and inspirational circumstances, such as those described in Chapter 5.

THE SUPERVISORY RELATIONSHIP

During the 1940s, trainees in the Infantry Officer Candidate School at Fort Benning, Georgia, were taught that "a leader is a person who can do everything his subordinates can, only better." Leaders in some civilian organizations still seem to subscribe to the same definition. In early America the straw boss was often the biggest or toughest person in the group—the one who could physically intimidate any member of the group. During the 1940s, supervisors in a factory in Arkansas were found guilty of whipping subordinates to keep them in line. Though corporal punishment, which seems extreme today, is not officially condoned, the Parent-Child values underlying it are still in evidence, and management by initmidation is still very much alive. Intimidation is not always physical; it may be accomplished with official authority through direct or veiled threats to the economic, professional, political, and social status of job incumbents.

During the early 1960s, supervisors at Texas Instruments became aware of the discrepancy between traditional supervisory practice and the participative approaches they were espousing in the company. A problem arose from the fact that standard textbook prescriptions did not provide guidelines for implementing the new practices with which they were experimenting. With the help of Training Director Earl Weed, about 12 first-level supervisors held a series of meetings for the purpose of removing ambiguity from their work roles. They developed two lists of guidelines—one descriptive of authority-oriented (Parent-Child) practices and the other descriptive of goal-oriented (Adult-Adult) leadership. These two lists are summarized in Exhibit 17.

The Parent-Child style of supervision in the left-hand column of Exhibit 17 is more likely to be practiced by supervisors with Theory X assumptions; the Adult-Adult behavior by supervisors operating from Theory Y assumptions.* Not all supervisors in the group that developed the Adult-Adult guidelines were Theory Y-oriented. However, even the Theory X types usually agreed intellectually that this was the more effective approach for getting results. The consensus of this group of supervisors illustrates the fact that deep-seated values (Parent tapes) are often subconscious and may be at variance with the conscious intellectual position. However, Theory X types who made deliberate attempts to apply the Adult-Adult approach began a gradual change in their values. After sustained application of the new approach, some of them ultimately became strongly supportive of Theory Y viewpoints.

The change from X to Y is a slow and difficult process, generally experienced in four phases: (1) awareness, (2) understanding, (3) commitment, and (4) habit. **Awareness** may occur as a result of a dramatic experience, an educational film or speech, reading a book, or simply through informal discussion. The awareness phase usually causes a person to become uneasy with the status quo or to see the advantage of another way of managing.

Understanding is usually the result of educational follow-up through reading, seminar participation, and further discussion. This is largely an

---

*See pp. 64-65 for definitions of McGregor's concepts of Theory X and Theory Y.

Parent-Child	Adult-Adult
1. Set clear goals for subordinates and define work methods for achieving them.	Participate with people in problem solving and goal setting and work with them in defining work methods.
2. Train subordinates in the knowledge, skills, and attitudes necessary for doing the job, enrolling them when necessary in appropriate training programs.	Optimize learning opportunities—choosing from options such as group problem solving and instruction by supervisors, peers, staff trainees, and programed instruction.
3. Let each person know what is expected of him or her in terms of well-defined standards of performance with regard to productivity and personal conduct.	Communicate customer and company requirements in terms of quality, schedules, costs, and constraints (financial, legal, time, policy) as a basis for group goal setting.
4. Evaluate each person's performance, acknowledge strong points, and give constructive criticism in terms of weaknesses to be overcome.	Involve people in defining performance and feedback criteria for self-evaluation of job effectiveness.
5. Apply immediate, consistent, and fair discipline to persons who step out of line.	Mediate conflict, explain rules and the consequences of violations, and make sure that disciplinary actions are fully understood.
6. Motivate people to do a good job by being enthusiastic and persuasive. Set an example through your own work habits.	Allow people to set challenging goals, and give them freedom to manage their own work.
7. Develop and install better work methods for the people in your group and monitor their use of these new methods.	Teach methods-improvement techniques to job incumbents through Work Simplification classes and by involving them with engineers and others in designing work systems.
8. Become familiar with your subordinates' strengths, limitations, and potential for development and give them career guidance and recommendations for improvement.	Let people take charge of their own careers by encouraging them to take the initiative in seeking vocational guidance, bidding on job openings, and enrolling in self-development programs.
9. Let people know you are watching them by praising them for their successful accomplishments and by punishing them for their failures.	Ensure performance feedback to job incumbents in a climate of candor that permits natural acknowledgment of success and discussion of failures.
10. Make most, if not all, of the decisions not covered by normal, everyday practices.	Encourage individuals and work groups to make decisions based on mututal goals.

Exhibit 17 Supervisory styles.

intellectual conditioning process in which the person may become an articulate spokesperson for a new theory, but in practice may continue to manage as before.

Commitment results from the realization that a discrepancy exists between theory and practice. For example, supervisors and union leaders may become enthused in a joint seminar on the merits of collaboration and commit themselves to a follow-up implementation program. If the new behavior is rewarding and encounters no insurmountable obstacles, implementation gradually becomes a more natural process.

Habit formation results gradually after sustained commitment has integrated the new process into a way of life in the workplace. From the awareness stage to habit formation is a long and difficult process requiring perhaps five to ten years. Some individuals make the transition rapidly, whereas others never progress beyond the understanding stage. Of course, a few persons are so firmly entrenched in tradition that they are psychologically blind to alternatives. These persons may never even reach the awareness stage, and the only viable recourse left to the organization is to reassign them, separate them from the work force, or encourage their early retirement.

EFFECTIVE TEAMS

McGregor's famous book *The Human Side of Enterprise** illustrates the theme that people's behavior reflects their values or attitudes. One type of attitude, which he called "Theory X," embodies a set of assumptions which, when translated into behavior, tends to bring out the worst in people. A contrasting attitude, which he labeled "Theory Y," provides more options for bringing out the best in people. Though the terminology of transactional analysis was not widely known when McGregor wrote his book, Theory X values are usually expressed as a Critical or Protective Parent in a Parent-Child relationship. Theory Y would generally find expression in Adult-Adult relationships, though at times, when appropriate, might also be expressed as Parent-Child, Adult-Child, and Child-Child transactions.

Individuals oriented toward Theory X seem to base their behavior on the following set of assumptions:

1. The average human being has an inherent dislike of work and will avoid it if possible.
2. Therefore, most people must be coerced, controlled, directed, and threatened with punishment to get them to put forth adequate effort toward the achievement of organizational objectives.
3. The average human prefers to be directed, wishes to avoid responsibility, has relatively little ambition, and wants security above all.

Individuals who think and act on the basis of Theory Y, whether deliberately or intuitively, subscribe to the following set of assumptions:

*Douglas McGregor, *The Human Side of Enterprise,* New York: McGraw-Hill, 1960.

1. The expenditure of physical and mental effort in work is as natural as play or rest.

2. External control and the threat of punishment are not the only means for bringing about effort toward organizational objectives. A person will exercise self-direction and self-control in the service of objectives to which she or he is committed.

3. Commitment to objectives is a function of the rewards associated with their achievement.

4. The average human being learns, under proper conditions, not only to accept but also to seek responsibility.

5. The capacity to exercise a relatively high degree of imagination, ingenuity, and creativity in the solution of organizational problems is widely, not narrowly, distributed in the population.

6. Under the conditions of modern industrial life, the intellectual potentialities of the average human being are only partially utilized.

In McGregor's discussion of the implications of Theory X and Theory Y, he noted that managerial behavior, practices, and systems rather commonly reflected Theory X assumptions. However, in research conducted by the MIT Sloan School of Management during the 1950s, it was found that the more successful organizations followed practices which were apparently based on Theory Y assumptions. For instance, with regard to the task-oriented group or team, such as a management-labor task force, it was observed that the successful group with a genuine unity of purpose tended to display certain characteristics.

Characteristics of Effective Groups

1. Climate. The "atmosphere," which can be sensed in a few minutes of observation, tends to be informal, comfortable, and relaxed. There are no obvious tensions. It is a working atmosphere in which people are involved and interested. There are no signs of boredom.

2. Discussion. There is a lot of discussion in which virtually everyone participates, but it remains pertinent to the task of the group. If the discussion gets off the subject, someone will bring it back in short order.

3. Goals. The task or the objective of the group is well understood and accepted by the members. There will have been free discussion of the objective at some point until it was formulated in such a way that the members of the group could commit themselves to it.

4. Listening. The members listen to one another! The discussion does not have the quality of jumping from one idea to another unrelated one. Every idea is given a hearing. People do not seem to be afraid of appearing foolish by putting forth a creative thought, even if it seems fairly extreme.

5. Disagreement. There is disagreement. The group is comfortable with this and shows no signs of having to avoid conflict or to keep everything on a plane of sweetness and light. Disagreements are not suppressed or overridden by premature group action. The reasons are carefully examined, and the group seeks to resolve them rather than to dominate the dissenter.

On the other hand, there is no "tyranny of the minority." Individuals who disagree do not appear to be trying to dominate the group or to express hostility. Their disagreement is an expression of a genuine difference of opinion, and they expect a hearing in order that a solution may be found. Sometimes there are basic disagreements which cannot be resolved. The group finds it possible to live with them, accepting them but not permitting them to block its efforts. Under some conditions, action will be deferred to permit further study of an issue among the members. On other occasions, where the disagreement cannot be resolved and action is necessary, it will be taken, but with open caution and recognition that the action may be subject to later reconsideration.

6. Consensus. Most decisions are reached by a kind of consensus in which it is clear that everybody is in general agreement and willing to go along. However, there is little tendency for individuals who oppose the action to keep their opposition private and thus let an apparent consensus mask real disagreement. Formal voting is at a minimum; the group does not accept a simple majority as a proper basis for action.

7. Criticism. Criticism is frequent, frank, and relatively comfortable. There is little evidence of personal attack, either openly or in a hidden fashion. The criticism has a constructive flavor in that it is oriented toward removing an obstacle that faces the group and prevents it from getting the job done.

8. Candor. People are free in expressing their feelings as well as their ideas, both on the problem and on the group's operation. There is little pussyfooting; there are few "hidden agendas." Everybody appears to know quite well how everybody else feels about any matter under discussion.

9. Action plan. When action is taken, clear assignments are made and accepted.

10. Chairmanship. The person chairing the group does not dominate it, nor on the contrary, does the group defer unduly to the leader. In fact, as one observes the activity, it is clear that the leadership shifts from time to time, depending on the circumstances. Different members, because of their knowledge or experience, are in a position at various times to act as "resources" for the group. The members utilize them in this fashion, and they occupy leadership roles while they are thus being used. There is little evidence of a struggle for power as the group operates. The issue is not who controls, but how to get the job done.

11. Feedback. The group is self-conscious about its own operations. Freqently, it will stop to examine how well it is doing or what may be interfering with its operation. The problem may be a matter of procedure, or it may be an individual whose behavior is interfering with the accomplishment of the group's objectives. Whatever it is, it gets open discussion until a solution is found.

Characteristics of Ineffective Groups

In studying the characteristics of groups that are relatively ineffective in accomplishing their purposes, McGregor reported the following characteristics.

1. Climate. The "atmosphere" is likely to reflect either indifference and boredom (people whispering to each other or carrying on side conversations, individuals who are obviously not involved, etc.) or tension (undercurrents of hostility and antagonism, stiffness and undue formality, etc.). The group is clearly not challenged by its task or genuinely involved in it.

2. Discussion. A few people tend to dominate the discussion. Often their contributions are way off the point. Little is done by anyone to keep the group clearly on the track.

3. Goals. From the things said, it is difficult to understand what the group task is or what its objectives are. These may have been stated by the chairman initially, but there is no evidence that the group either understands or accepts a common objective. On the contrary, it is usually evident that different people have different, private, and personal objectives which they are attempting to achieve in the group, and these are often in conflict with one another and with the group's task.

4. Listening. People do not really listen to one another. Ideas are ignored and overridden. The discussion jumps around with little coherence and no sense of movement along a track. One gets the impression that there is much talking for effect—people make speeches which are obviously intended to impress someone else rather than being relevant to the task at hand. Conversation with members after the meeting will reveal that they have failed to express ideas or feelings which they may have had for fear they would be criticized or regarded as silly. Some members feel that the leader or the other members are constantly making judgments of them in terms of evaluations of the contributions they make, and so they are extremely careful about what they say.

5. *Disagreement.* Disagreements are generally not dealt with effectively by the group. They may be completely suppressed by a leader who fears conflict. On the other hand, they may result in open warfare, the consequence of which is domination by one subgroup over another. They may be "resolved" by a vote in which a very small majority wins the day and a large minority remains completely unconvinced.

There may be a "tyranny of the minority" in which an individual or a small subgroup is so aggressive that the majority accedes in order to preserve the peace or to get on with the task. In general, only the more aggressive members get their ideas considered, because the less aggressive people tend either to keep quiet altogether or to give up after short, ineffectual attempts to be heard.

6. *Consensus.* Actions are often taken prematurely before the real issues are either examined or resolved. There will be much grousing after the meeting by people who disliked the decision but failed to speak up about it in the meeting itself. A simple majority is considered sufficient for action, and the minority is expected to go along. Most of the time, however, the minority remains resentful and uncommitted to the decision.

7. *Criticism.* Criticism may be present, but it is embarrassing and tension producing. It often appears to involve personal hostility, and the members are uncomfortable with this and unable to cope with it. Criticism of ideas tends to be destructive. Sometimes every idea proposed will be "clobbered" by someone else. In such situations, no one will be willing to take the risk of offering an idea.

8. *Candor.* Personal feelings are hidden rather than brought out in the open. The general attitude of the group is that feelings are inappropriate for discussion and would be too explosive if brought out on the table.

9. *Action plan.* Action decisions tend to be unclear; no one really knows who is going to do what. Even when assignments of responsibility are made, there is often considerable doubt as to whether they will be carried out.

10. *Chairmanship.* The leadership remains clearly with the committee chairman. This person may be weak or strong, but she or he always sits "at the head of the table."

11. *Feedback.* The group tends to avoid any objective discussion of how it is functioning as a group. There is often much discussion after the meeting of what went wrong and why, but these matters are seldom brought up and considered within the meeting itself, where they might be resolved.

How a Group Measures Its Effectiveness

The principles elaborated above regarding the functioning of effective and ineffective groups can serve as guidelines for helping a group give itself feedback on how well it is doing as a group. Exhibit 18 summarizes these criteria in a group feedback form. The recommended use of this form is to have a supply of them on hand, and when a meeting seems not to be functioning as desired, stop and have each member complete a form. The group average or median for each item is the score for that item. Similarly, a highly successful meeting might be followed by self-assessment in the same manner. The potentially perfect score for the whole form is 99, and the absolute low is zero.

	0 1 2 3 4 5 6 7 8 9	
1. Climate	0 1 2 3 4 5 6 7 8 9	
	indifference, boredom	involvement, interest
2. Discussion	0 1 2 3 4 5 6 7 8 9	
	unbalanced, irrelevant	widespread, relevant
3. Goals	0 1 2 3 4 5 6 7 8 9	
	unclear, conflicting	understood, accepted
4. Listening	0 1 2 3 4 5 6 7 8 9	
	ideas ignored, overridden	attentive, respectful
5. Disagreement	0 1 2 3 4 5 6 7 8 9	
	conflict suppressed, open warfare, or tyranny of the minority	thoughtful acceptance of conflict, rational expression of difference
6. Consensus	0 1 2 3 4 5 6 7 8 9	
	premature action, resentful minority(ies)	working through to agreement
7. Criticism	0 1 2 3 4 5 6 7 8 9	
	tension-producing, personal attacks	obstacle-directed discussion
8. Candor	0 1 2 3 4 5 6 7 8 9	
	hidden feelings	free expression of feelings
9. Action plan	0 1 2 3 4 5 6 7 8 9	
	unclear assignments, uncommitted acceptance	clear, accepted assignments
10. Chairmanship	0 1 2 3 4 5 6 7 8 9	
	domineering, arbitrary, Parent-Child	democratic, thoughtful, Adult-Adult
11. Feedback	0 1 2 3 4 5 6 7 8 9	
	fault finding after meeting	self-examination during meeting

Exhibit 18 Group feedback form.

In practice, groups don't hit these extremes, but a well-functioning group scores above 75 and a poorly functioning group below 50.

PERFORMANCE REVIEW

It is customary in many organizations to conduct periodic formal performance appraisals. The avowed purpose of performance appraisal is to assess the performance of the individual and to communicate the results of this evaluation to the individual, along with suggestions for improvement.

During the 1950s, Douglas McGregor took what he called an "uneasy look at performance appraisal"* and noted that the judgmental aspects of ratings, particulary when they appeared to be administered on the basis of Theory X assumptions, tended to undermine the developmental potential of the performance-review process. As real human development is self-inspired and self-directed, traditional performance appraisals undermine self-development by incurring conformity, rebellion, and hostility. Though some individuals improve their job performance as a result of advice from the supervisor, the value of the improved performance might be outweighed by the increased dependency of the individual on the boss for the next steps in his or her development. The individual not only finds an apron string which relieves him or her of the responsibility for self-development, but also acquires a model for development which encourages the person, in turn, to meddle with the self-development of people whose performance is being reviewed.

This is not to say that performance appraisals are not needed and that supervisors should not have a role in them. Performance appraisals are in process continuously, informally if not formally, in terms of both self-appraisal and evaluations by others. The supervisor, as a member of a natural work group, has a key role in the performance-appraisal process. But this role, if it is to result in personal and professional development, is through an Adult-Adult rather than a Parent-Child relationship.

Supervisors who act as self-appointed missionaries for "shaping up the troops" commonly resort to criticism as the basis for bringing about improved performance. The term "criticism," as used here, refers to evaluations, advice, warnings, admonitions, threats, and other judgmental information transmitted by someone of higher authority to someone of lower authority. Criticism among peers, when undertaken as a deliberate and candid feedback process, may serve a constructive role. However, the same information from someone higher in the "chain of command" seldom affords the ratee opportunity for candid discussion or unfiltered rebuttal. Hence the ratee characteristically masks resentment and hostility with a veneer of a smile and while appearing to show gratitude for the well-meant criticism, covertly puts the supervisor on the top of his or her "to be killed" list.

---

*Douglas McGregor, "An Uneasy Look at Performance Appraisal" (HBR Classic), *Harvard Business Review* (May-June 1957 and September-October 1972).

Successful performance and continuing improvement require feedback. The term "feedback," as used here, refers to an Adult-Adult way of giving help; it is a corrective process through which individuals can learn how well their behavior matches their intentions.* Feedback, at its best, is:

1. Timely—usually immediate.

2. Descriptive rather than evaluative.

3. Specific rather than general.

4. Sensitive to the needs of the receiver as well as the sender.

5. Directed toward controllable behavior.

6. Solicited rather than imposed.

7. Tested for accuracy with the receiver(s).

Compare, for example, the consequences of criticism and feedback in the following situation. Harry Brown, supervisor of the maintenance department, receives three telephone calls within one week complaining about the performance of Roy Johnson, one of the general maintenance men in his department. The essence of the three calls was reflected in a call from James Smith, production foreman: "Harry, I called to report on the performance of Roy Johnson from your department who repaired the bottling machine in my shop this morning. I guess you could say I have good news and bad news. The good news is that he repaired the equipment and got it on stream in record time. The bad news is that he antagonized my operators to the point that they wanted to throw him out. They've been talking to the shop steward trying to drum up a grievance. The steward advised me to keep Johnson out of the department or there will be union action for sure the next time."

"I'm sorry to hear this, Jim, but I appreciate your call. Yours is not the first complaint. Can you give me a few more details about Roy's behavior that caused this problem?"

"It's his way of approaching the job—he acts like a know-it-all and treats my people as though the breakdown was all their fault. He wouldn't give them a civil answer to their questions about the cause of the problem and as much as told them to tend to their business of operating the machines—that maintenance was not in their job descriptions. Moreover, he insinuated that if they learned how to operate the equipment properly, they wouldn't have so many breakdowns."

Harry Brown has thus received feedback about the unsatisfactory performance of Roy Johnson. What does he do now? Does he wait until performance-review time and unload on Roy a detailed list of failures, shortcomings, and weaknesses, with admonitions to "shape up" if he wants to

---

*For further information on feedback, *see* David A. Kolb, Irwin M. Rubin, and James M. McIntyre, *Organizational Psychology—An Experiential Approach*, 2d ed., Englewood Cliffs, N.J.: Prentice-Hall 1974.

"succeed in this organization"? Should he approach Roy obliquely with the sandwich technique, starting his discussion with a compliment about his high-quality workmanship and then, when Roy is experiencing a rosy glow from these positive strokes, let him have it between the eyes with a criticism? Then does he conclude the interview with a compliment to try to end on a positive note? Or does he call Roy in at the first offense and "chew him out" to make sure it doesn't happen again?

These approaches may or may not result in improving Roy's performance, depending on the quality of the relationship between Harry and Roy. Also, the success of these approaches depends to a high degree on Roy's values and expectations. If Roy were a submissive conformist, which Smith's complaint suggests he is not, he might comply obediently with Harry's admonitions. But if Roy is a member of the swelling ranks of employees who resent the officious use of authority, he might covertly or even openly put Harry on his "to be killed" list.

However, Harry is an experienced supervisor and knows that if Roy does not take part in formulating the change process, he is not likely to be committed to any changes essential to his success. If any change takes place as a result of edict, it is likely to be in the form of defensive, subversive, or aggressive behavior fueled by the normal hostility usually generated by Parent-Child treatment.

If Harry avoids the Parent-Child approach of criticism and employs instead the Adult-Adult approach of feedback, he might involve Roy in the change process and hence be more likely to secure Roy's commitment to change.

Using the seven characteristics of feedback enumerated above, Harry decides that it would be timely to talk to Roy immediately rather than wait until performance review. He might set up the encounter by saying, "Roy, when you have about 30 minutes when you can break away from your work, could we get together?"

In the ensuing discussion, Harry comes straight to the second point and says, "Roy, I received three phone calls about you this week, and in each case they had both good and bad things to say about your work." Note that Harry is not making value judgments, but rather is describing the events that prompted the meeting. Roy is, of course, interested in the information and should be given an opportunity to speak up and perhaps satisfy point six by asking Harry what the people had to say.

Going on to point three, to be descriptive rather than general, Harry says, "In two cases they were complimentary about the quality of your work and the speed with which you completed the job, but in all three cases they said that something you said or did antagonized the people around you—that you were not courteous or friendly and that you acted as though you were better than they were. What do you suppose could have caused them to feel that way?" Note that Harry is still avoiding the expression of value judgments and is being as specific as he can be without violating confidences and that he is giving Roy an opportunity to express his feelings. He is sensitive to the understandable defensiveness which Roy is probably experiencing and also to Roy's pride in his competence as a craftsman. Hence he is satisfying point four by considering the needs of Roy as the receiver as well as his own obligation to convey information to Roy as the first step toward changing his behavior.

Roy expresses his feelings by saying, "It's hard to be courteous and polite to a bunch of fatheads who don't know how to use their equipment properly. That bottling machine is beautifully engineered equipment, and any dimwit could keep it going. If you ask me, they are deliberately sabotaging it just so they can get a little downtime. They don't deserve courteous treatment. Their supervisor's too soft on them—they need someone like me who's not afraid to tell 'em off."

Harry doesn't disagree with Roy, but says, "In the meantime, the people are jumping on *me*. I guess I'm asking you for your help in getting them off my back. They say that they don't want you in their shop. Yet you are one of the most technically competent persons in the maintenance department. But how am I going to meet *my* responsibility if top technicians like you aren't wanted on repair jobs?" Note that Harry is still respecting Roy's feelings, but he is building up to let Roy address himself to point five—altering controllable behavior. He recognizes that he can't successfully change Roy through threats, persuasion, bribery, or manipulation—that Roy's behavior will change only if he himself decides to change it.

Roy's response states, in effect, "Harry, I'm sorry they're giving *you* a hard time. I guess they're too chicken to say anything to me. But it's not your fault. For your sake I'll try to do better in the future, but it's not going to be easy. If there's anything I can't stand, it's fatheads who neglect their equipment."

Harry replies to Roy by saying, "I appreciate your help on this, Roy, and I think I know just how you feel about people who seem to be careless with equipment. But it's not just for me, it's also for you. Your career is tied to your ability to get along with people just as strongly as it's related to your technical competence. In the meantime, if someone else tries to give me a hard time about you, what'll I tell them?"

"Tell them not to jump to conclusions—that maybe I wasn't feeling good that day and that it won't happen again. Hell, I wasn't trying to start a war; I didn't know they'd take it so seriously. But I'll take it easy on them in the future. Hey, I've got to run now, it's almost three, and I promised I'd help them in the packaging department." Note that Harry is satisfying point seven by testing the accuracy of his feedback by asking Roy to define the corrective action he plans to take.

Because job performance is continuous, performance appraisal too must be continuous. Some critics snipe at periodic performance appraisals on the basis that six-month or annual reviews are not realistically keyed to the continuous and sporadic nature of work. This criticism of periodic reviews is valid if they are the only reviews conducted. It is true that performance appraisal and feedback should be continuous and timely; however, the function of the periodic review is different from, but a necessary adjunct to, the ongoing review. The day-to-day process is essential to deal with situations such as the example above involving a maintenance supervisor and a maintenance technician in his work group. However, the periodic review also serves a vital function by affording an opportunity for individuals to: (1) review accomplishments, (2) establish goals, (3) agree on priorities, and (4) coordinate work plans with others. In other words, the periodic review usually establishes six- to twelve-month goals which serve as a foundation for planning and assessing near-term activities.

The Adult-Adult periodic review process ideally builds on prework by a natural work group. For example, a department head, in planning the charter for the coming year, might lead his or her natural work group in an off-site, two-day workshop for defining departmental goals and strategies. Having reached consensus on the departmental charter, each member, through choice or assignment, assumes ownership of a chunk of the departmental mission. Responsibilities assumed at this stage are tentative, pending ratification of the proposed departmental charter in the upcoming divisional planning conference.

The individual performance-appraisal process is then launched from the ratified departmental charter. The department head activates the performance-review process by distributing a review form to each person in the work group to answer three basic questions:

1. What were your major achievements during the past six months?
2. What are your goals for the next six months?
3. What are your long-term goals?

Answers to these three questions are usually summarized on a single sheet of paper by each job incumbent, who returns the completed form to his or her immediate supervisor.

After reviewing the completed form, the supervisor consults the person regarding a mutually convenient time to hold the performance-review discussion. A supervisor who is sensitive to the symbolism of organizational rank will attempt to hold the meeting away from his or her own office— perhaps in the job incumbent's office or a nearby conference room. If the meeting is held in the supervisor's office, the supervisor will avoid the "throne-behind-the-desk" posture and will also take measures to ensure privacy and to prevent interruptions.

The most developmental interviews are conducted by supervisors who approach the performance-review discussion with a mental set to do more listening than talking. Supervisors gain competence for this role through insights and skills gained through transactional analysis and conference leadership so that the natural use of feedback (rather than criticism) establishes the climate for the discussion. Though constructive discussions are facilitated through the application of these principles, it is important that the supervisor maintain an authentic relationship by not departing too radically from his or her everyday style.

After opening the discussion—usually with small talk—the supervisor may take a cue from the job incumbent in deciding whether to open the business discussion by asking a question or whether to follow a course initiated by the other person through a question or comment. If the supervisor begins the discussion, she or he may acknowledge the enumerated achievements and ask, "In looking over your achievements, Jane, how do you feel about them?" The supervisor is neither in a rush to get a response nor afraid of silence, but rather is prepared to wait to give Jane an opportunity to warm up to the question. The supervisor may wish to follow this initial discussion with another question: "Now that you've had the benefit of this experience, Jane, if you were doing this over again, is there anything you'd do differently?" Again, the supervisor waits, even if Jane doesn't answer immediately. Or, the supervisor might say, "You had a major hand in opening our new production line. I'll bet you learned a lot from that experience." Again, the necessary pause for Jane's response. Or, "John Smith is going to Charleston to start up operations in our new South Carolina plant. If he asked you for advice, what would you say?"

Jane's answer might be, "It's funny you should ask that question, 'cause if I were doing it over, I'd do three things differently." Jane then proceeds to detail a better approach to her accomplishments of the past six months.

The initial and primary focus of the supervisor's role is to get the job incumbent to assume the responsibility for reviewing and assessing his or her own accomplishments. If the job incumbent is under the false illusion of having accomplished goals adequately, this may be the fault of the supervisor for having failed to give timely and valid feedback. Or, it may be a result of the supervisor's failure to help the job incumbent establish well-defined goals and acceptable criteria of achievements through which to assess his or her own performance.

Having reviewed achievements and lessons learned through them, they can move on to goals to be accomplished. Jointly they establish short- and long-range goal priorities and strategies for achieving them and define their individual and mutual roles in attaining and measuring accomplishments. The supervisor does not pull rank on the job incumbent by overriding the latter's viewpoint. However, the supervisor may have information to share with the job incumbent in terms of constraints imposed by budgets, schedules, policy, laws, and customer commitments. When the job incumbent and supervisor are on the same data base, they can arrive at decisions through consensus in an

Adult-Adult style. When agreement is reached, they adjourn, the job incumbent taking the form to modify it according to their agreement. The individual makes any necessary changes, duplicates the form, gives one to the supervisor and retains a copy for his or her six-month charter.

After completing this one-on-one meeting with all individuals, the supervisor convenes them for a joint session. Each person in turn reports to the total group his or her goals and strategies as a basis for planning collaborative efforts and avoiding conflicts and redundancies.

Though the periodic performance review establishes a six-month charter, it usually needs interim updating. After the forms are completed and discussed, the supervisor may consult the group to choose monthly two-hour meeting dates for updating the charters. In these monthly meetings, each person reports on achievements, obstacles, breakthroughs, new assignments, setbacks, problems, and opportunities. These meetings keep the group updated and provide opportunity for members to help one another through suggestions and collaborative effort.

Thus when the next review period arrives, there are no surprises. Under such a system, each person is continuously accountable for his or her goals and achievements and the measurement of his or her own performance. Though this may be the period of awarding the discretionary bonus or giving notice of termination, such actions come as no surprise to persons reporting to supervisors who apply the principles of feedback enumerated earlier. To the extent that the individual and the supervisor are on the same data base, allegations of favoritism, unfairness, and arbitrariness are less likely to be made.

When performance reviews are not taken seriously at lower job-grade levels, it's usually because they are not appropriately initiated and supported at the higher levels. Vice-presidents may protest that their charters are established by the annual planning conference and hence see no need to duplicate them with the performance-review procedure used at lower levels. These protestors may fail to realize that the primary purpose of performance review at their level is not to establish charters, but rather to initiate the system to be used at successively lower levels. The vice-president's use of the form with the department heads is a language of action which says, in effect, "performance reviews are important." Moreover, successfully conducted performance reviews at the upper levels serve as models which persons at lower levels tend to emulate.

Goal-oriented performance appraisals traditionally do not include the hourly paid employees. The reasoning supporting this tradition is that wage-roll people are paid to carry out orders—not to set goals. Moreover, members of the bargaining unit are presumed to have their responsibilities prescribed by a standard job description. Based on such an assumption, performance reviews for the hourly work force tend to be Parent-Child merit-rating systems. However, perceptive managers are finding that traditional practice and assumptions provide inappropriate guidelines for dealing with members of the new work ethic and are beginning to innovate Adult-Adult performance-review systems which have equal relevance for salaried and wage-roll people.

The goal-oriented performance review described above can be adapted to hourly workers if it is appropriately keyed to their job constraints. When hourly workers comprise interdependent members of a work team, it may be appropriate to administer the system on a group basis. In this case, the first-level supervisor may convene the work group in a conference room, distribute the forms to them, and lead them through the goal-setting process. Using a flip chart or chalk board, the supervisor involves them in compiling a list of their group's six-month achievements. Such a list may be narrowed to the most important achievements, which each records on his or her performance-review form. In a similar manner, the supervisor involves the group in defining goals, following the problem-solving goal-setting principles described in Chapter 2. Thus each person now has a list of the group's achievements and goals on his or her form. This group process has now paved the way for involving each person in a one-on-one discussion.

The supervisor arranges for a private meeting with each member of the group, asking them each to bring the completed form to the meeting. To make the process nonthreatening to the traditional, and worthwhile to the free-thinkers, the supervisor might say, "Bring this completed form to the meeting, as it will be the basis for much of our discussion. By the way, if any of you wish to add some of your personal achievements or goals to those we have listed as a group, feel free to do so—I'll be glad to discuss them with you."

In the ensuing one-on-one discussions, the supervisor strives to do more listening than talking, to apply the Adult-Adult process of feedback, and to avoid Parent-Child expressions of criticism, condescension, and direction. Also, as in the case of the salaried personnel, the supervisor should schedule interim meetings to keep the group updated, to involve them in the changes which invariably occur in a work place, and to enable them to keep their goals updated.

Controversy continues to rage over the issue of whether or not the performance-review discussion of goals and achievements should include a discussion of pay. The traditional Parent-Child (Theory X) viewpoint holds that they should be separated on the basis that money is an emotion-arousing subject which would impair the logical and deliberate process of goal setting. The assumption behind this viewpoint is that a disappointing pay adjustment would demotivate people from setting and pursuing challenging goals. The Adult-Adult (Theory Y) position is that people like to understand the relationship between their accomplishments and the reward systems of the organization. Pay, being one of the more tangible forms of feedback from the supervisor, is an integral part of the performance review. Needless to say, the better the individual understands the criteria by which he or she as an individual is appraised and the technicalities of wage and salary administration, the less likely that person is to be surprised and turned off by the subject of compensation during performance review. To use the analogy of the baseball game, adult players don't blame the umpire when they strike out, nor do they expect the umpire to give them special consideration or tell them how to improve their game. In contrast, immature players more often do try to blame the umpire or others for their failures. A nurturing umpire who attempted to assume a helping role would only perpetuate this immaturity. People are more likely to act like adults when they are treated like adults.

In summary, performance review at its worst tends to incur outrage, intimidation, and disengagement. At its best, it is an Adult feedback process that helps people take charge of their own careers and organizational responsibilities.

Chapter 5

Interrupting
the Win-Lose Cycle

Union leaders and managers alike tend to scoff at the idea that members of the other party could be rational and open-minded about, or even desirous of, trying to work together in harmony. Each will cite specific and numerous incidents to illustrate the hostility, irrationality, and untrustworthiness of the other. Each side has internalized the Parent tape articulated a century earlier by Samuel Gompers to the effect that management and labor have separate and conflicting goals. So strongly entrenched and commonly accepted is the adversary relationship that any unilateral act of affirmation by the one is automatically viewed by the other with suspicion. A friendly and respectful act by one usually results in speculation as to the real motive behind it and a hostile response to the presumed ulterior motive.

But an outsider, not organizationally associated with either party, may find members of either party to be rational, cooperative, and friendly. This is not to say that these congenial individuals do not harbor cultural prejudices toward members of the other gender or of other races, nationalities, religions, and political parties. However, these polarizations are usually secondary to their orientation in the management-labor dichotomy. Hence prejudiced white male Republican Protestants might unite with black Catholics or female Jewish Democrats if such alliances serve to strengthen the clout of their labor or management group.

CRISIS SHARING

Members of both parties typically proceed on their characteristic adversary course as though it were the natural and inevitable order of things. However, should a condition threaten the survival of the organization, its adversary members may cease hostilities and rally collaboratively to the higher-priority common cause of survival.

For instance, the birth of the Scanlon plan itself was the result of a crisis facing a steel mill in the 1930s. When it was clear that the business could go under, the local steelworkers' union, under Joseph Scanlon's leadership, agreed to cooperate to improve productivity. The workers agreed not to ask for higher wages and to collaborate in reducing costs, decreasing waste, improving efficiency, and raising quality. This cooperation paid off within a few months; the company survived and eventually was able to improve wages and working conditions.

In 1975 the Federal Mediation and Conciliation Service (FMCS) introduced a "Relationship by Objectives" (RBO) intervention process, which is proving effective in dealing with crisis situations between management and labor. Though RBO applies advanced conflict-resolution techniques, it is conducted in the language of the local union committeepeople and supervisors from the shop floor where the crises are initiated. It involves plant-level union representatives and managers rather than representatives of international union headquarters and company board rooms in the crisis-resolution process.

John Popular, as Associate Director for Technical Services, FMCS, described the typical approach implemented by RBO:

> RBO is a down-to-earth approach. Theories are pushed aside, and representatives from both sides are asked to roll up their sleeves, identify the problems in their relationship and in their expectations of it, and develop the means to solve them.
>
> The groups are first divided into three or four teams, with each team composed of labor and management members and mediator. Each team is asked to respond to the question: "What do you expect to gain from this program?"
>
> Next, the teams are shown a movie "Barney and Clyde (Or You Can't Negotiate an Attitude)," produced by the FMCS. This 22-minute film dramatizes a contract negotiation in which poor attitudes on the shop floor spill over into the negotiations. After viewing the film, the teams are asked to:
>
> —Analyze the attitudes of the supervisor and the union steward;
> —List the problems in the company-union relationship depicted in the film;
> —Recommend how to improve the relationship.
>
> After each team exercise, the whole group reassembles to discuss their reports. Up to this point, the process is an exercise in group dynamics, an attempt to stimulate the participants' thinking, and an important psychological groundwork to the program itself. The participants begin to associate their observations of "Barney and Clyde" with their own situtaion.
>
> Then the RBO program separates the group into labor and management components. In separate conferences, the participants are asked to respond to these questions:
>
> —What should the other party be doing to improve labor-management relations?
> —What should you be doing?

The responses are collected and similar answers are consolidated. Negative complaints are restated as positive goals. The mediators then draw up four lists:

1. According to the company, the union should. . . .
2. According to the company, the company should. . . .
3. According to the union, the company should. . . .
4. According to the union, the union should. . . .

This ends the first RBO phase.

In step two, labor and management meet together to review the four lists to narrow the selection of mutually agreeable objectives. Although there are numerous variations, almost all the goals touch on:

—Labor-management communications;
—Management attitudes and practices;
—Union attitudes and practices;
—Training.

In the third step, the entire group is asked to consolidate the lists into a single list of mutual objectives. This is broken into four parts, with each part assigned to one of the original teams for study. The teams must develop action steps to accomplish the objectives. Then management and union groups meet again in separate conferences to review the team proposals and to formulate specific action steps for attaining the objectives on which the two sides have already agreed.

In the next-to-last step, the entire group reassembles to hammer out differences. Finally, a review of the goals, action steps, and assignments of responsibility is made and a timetable for resolution of the problems is adopted.

The RBO process does not end with this concentrated seminar format: automatic 90-day follow-ups are conducted. Here, FMCS mediators track the progress of the new labor-management mechanisms—based on changed attitudes and a spirit of more mutual trust and participation. If necessary, additional advice and counsel are offered.*

Of the 18 RBO programs undertaken initially, all are claimed to have achieved varying degrees of success. In addition to interrupting crises, RBO applications have caused grievance and arbitration case loads to drop to less than one-half their previous levels. Moreover, the RBO experience creates a problem-solving environment conducive to resolving daily issues which might otherwise balloon into win-lose conflicts. Popular quotes from a letter to FMCS by Ron Carey, president of Teamsters Local 804, representing 6000 union members at United Parcel Service: "Your program and personnel have helped to remove difficult built-in labor relations obstacles. . . .I congratulate you and the entire staff for pointing out that there must be a better way."

---

*John J. Popular, "U.S. Mediators Try to Build Common Objectives," *World of Work Report,* Vol. 1, No. 7, Work in America Institute, September 1976, pp. 1-3. Reprinted by permission.

Crisis sharing, unfortunately, is somewhat of a last-ditch effort to be activated only under conditions of dire emergency—when the welfare of all members is imminently at stake. Actually, members of any organization have a joint stake in its success, no matter how healthy it may be, but it may take a crisis to sensitize them to that fact. Any viable organization is made more productive when all members pull together on the basis of their joint stake. Unfortunately, the nature of this joint stake is usually not understood or believed by its members; hence they have little incentive to go all out for improving productivity. In many cases, particularly in the public sector, members see little relationship between organizational effectiveness and their level of compensation. Moreover, since managers often cry "wolf," while their organizations continue to survive and meet union wage demands, it is understandable if union members come to disbelieve company pronouncements. If a real crisis of organizational survival does arise, conditioned cynicism may actually permit the organization to founder.

The problem, of course, is that the data base from which management operates is not typically shared with members of the bargaining units. Consequently, it is understandable if they perceive the goals and reward systems of the organizaiton to be arbitrarily controlled by "management." By the same token, management seldom has a deep appreciation of the problems facing the union and its membership. The mission, then, is to get the union and management on a common data base without waiting for or creating a crisis to bring it about.

IN-HOUSE CONFRONTATION

Collaborative efforts stemming from informal and serendipitous relationships within the organization are sometimes more successful than preplanned and contrived efforts. Formal proposals of collaboration by management to the union are almost certain to be rejected. But if a representative of management, who is trusted by a representative of the union, should in an informal discussion make such a suggestion, it might be given serious consideration. For instance, a personnel director of a supermarket chain who had established a friendly rapport with a key union representative was asked during one of their informal discussions, "What have you been doing to your supervisors?" "Why do you ask?" responded the personnel director. "Because they're not as bad as they used to be," replied the union representative. This conversation led to a discussion of the training program in which the supervisors had participated during the past year.

Because of his union friend's expressed interest in the program, the personnel director asked him if he would like to participate in one of the supervisory training programs. The union leader said that he would, but needed to clear it with the business representative in the union's international headquarters. The Retail Clerks International Union not only gave him permission, but also suggested that the opportunity be provided to other union leaders. In due course, 20 union representatives participated in the company's management training program.

The course proved to be as relevant to the union leaders as it was to the company managers. It enabled them to observe and classify their own behavior and motives; it pointed up the futility and wastefulness of the win-lose strategy which had characterized their relationship to management and sometimes to each other. Hence following the formal training process, they were cautiously willing to consider the personnel director's suggestion that they participate in a management-labor confrontation to begin breaking down the traditional barriers to cooperation. It should be noted that their trust in the personnel director who coordinated these efforts was a key element in obtaining their participation.

The two parties—eight members of top management and eight leaders of their local unions—met in an off-site conference room. The personnel director, as conference leader, opened the meeting by reviewing its purpose: to discover ways to begin working together toward common goals. He noted that in talking individually to each person in the room, all had endorsed the principle that the success of the organization would benefit each conference participant and all members of the organization. He also reported that members of both parties deplored union-management warfare because it wasted so much talent and time and that both parties were willing to work toward a strategy of cooperation for pursuing their mutual goals.

As a result of their earlier involvement in the common training program, the participants no longer looked on conflict as something to be avoided or suppressed. Rather, they now understand it to be inevitable and as a medium for reaching consensus.

The two parties were given a three-step assignment. In the first step each group, working separately, was to define what its members saw as the soundest possible relationship which would enable management and the union to work together cooperatively.

To satisfy this first step, each group developed lists of its own roles and the other party's roles in the ideal relationship. Typical role descriptions suggested by managers included the following:

Management should:

1. Maintain open communications with the union on company goals and objectives, economics of the industry and company, distribution of company profits, and problems facing the company.

2. Participate in prebargaining discussions to define the current economic climate, understand employee attitudes and concerns, assess the strengths and weaknesses of the present contract, and identify possible obstacles to effective negotiations.

3. Create more opportunity for joint problem solving through job enrichment, administration of benefit programs, training processes, and safety programs.

The union should:

1. Develop a better understanding of the nature of the company business.
2. Develop understanding of the relationship of productivity to wages and benefits.
3. Recognize the consequences of taking a fixed position—the win-lose trap.
4. Subdue personal interests to overall company and union objectives.
5. Accept responsibility to communicate facts to employees without prejudice.

Typical descriptions of the ideal relationship offered by the union officials:

Management should:

1. Take action on complaints, grievances, and questions without needless delay.
2. Provide a uniform education program for all supervisors on interpreting and applying the contract.
3. Consult employees on changes in work schedules, shifts, transfers, location, and so on.
4. Rate employees by uniform and fair criteria so employees know where they stand.
5. Coordinate supervisors between departments to prevent needless costs and wastes.

The union should:

1. Communicate problems, complaints, and contract infractions to management.
2. Represent all employees fairly.
3. Have access to top management without getting the "runaround" at lower levels.
4. Be concerned with costs and the amount of production.
5. See that employees are correctly rated for skills they have and are paid for jobs they do.

The second step was to define the actual relationship existing between management and the union. Descriptions like the following came from company executives.

Management:

1. Does not communicate adequately.
2. Does not listen effectively to what the union tries to say.
3. Has insufficient concern for the union's view.
4. Looks for political implications in union actions.
5. Fails to follow through on promises.
6. Gives inconsistent interpretations of union agreements and company policies.
7. Does not encourage first-level supervisors to be responsive.

The union:

1. Is interested only in political and personal gain.
2. Is unconcerned with the company's need to increase productivity.
3. Yields too easily to employee pressure.
4. Makes unrealistic initial demands in collective bargaining, raising undue aspirations among employees.
5. Is unaware of the company's financial and competitive situation.

Union officials described actual union-company relationships as follows:

Management:

1. Does not trust intentions of union officers.
2. Is sincere at the top levels, but people at the lower levels do not care about basic improvements in industrial relations.
3. Is afraid to, or is incapable of, making decisions at the first level.

The union:

1. Has sincere convictions and honest intentions.
2. Is concerned with saving company money.
3. Represents the thinking of its total membership.
4. Would rather solve problems than impose demands on the company.

This second step resulted in much discussion and "leveling" as problems were identified and clarified. As more information surfaced, members of each group could see the validity or basis of each other's allegations.

At this point the two groups were ready to take the third step, which was to plan changes that would lead to the best possible relationship between management and the union. The members jointly identified areas of basic disagreement and separately ranked ideas for change in terms of importance for improving the relationship. Here again, they encountered conflict that had to be resolved.

Management had given top priority to the development of a prebargaining session that would result in the candid exchange of information between management and the union before formal negotiations were begun. Union officers agreed with the importance of this strategy, but felt that some unfinished business regarding employee benefits had to be resolved first. They pointed out that their constituents were looking forward to some tangible results from these sessions and that the consummation of the long-pending revision of an insurance plan and other company benefit programs would serve this purpose.

Although these benefits were not perceived by management to be first in importance, both parties agreed that they had to be dealt with first in order to pave the way for discussion of more imortant, longer-range issues. So the issues were handled in that order. Thus the parties were able to develop a prebargaining procedure that would enable them to go into formal collective bargaining with a relatively clean slate—without secret agendas to put each other on the defensive.

Significantly, when the personnel director and his associates later developed the Team Improvement Laboratory in the company for enriching jobs and developing employee talents, the program had the full support of the union.* Both management and the union would plan their meetings to avoid conflicts with each other's schedules.

The involvement of employees in managing their jobs and in interpreting the results of attitude surveys surfaced many problems to be solved to avoid their becoming issues for grievances and collective bargaining. As a result, collective bargaining as a formal process usually has been concluded in a single day since the program got under way.

So strong is the alliance between the local union leadership and the company management that when the international union called an industrywide strike involving five major food chains in that region, employees of the company failed to heed the strike call and remained on the job, though the other four companies were struck. Their decision was not influenced by last-minute counterstrike intervention by management, but was a result of the feeling that they had a joint stake with management in the enterprise.

Though the ultimate company-union relationship became firmly established on a foundation of mutual trust and collaborative effort, the fact remains that its beginning was spawned by the tenuous relationship of two individuals and the improbable approval of the union business representative when the personnel director made his first overture at involvement.

THE PUBLIC SEMINAR

For several years the author has conducted annual one-day orientation seminars on union-management cooperation in the Chicago area. The

---

*Irving Borwick, "Team Improvement Laboratory," *Personnel Journal* (January 1969): 18-24; *also* M. Scott Myers, *Every Employee a Manager*, New York: McGraw-Hill, 1970, pp. 87-95.

brochure encourages the enrollment of members of both management and labor, even to the point of offering tuition reductions to organizations which are so represented. But in most cases a company's first enrollments include only managers, who enroll for the purpose of assessing the program and determining whether or not it is "safe" to bring union representatives to future programs.

Two factors coalesce to lead some managers to believe that it is desirable to include union members in future seminars. One is the fact that the program does not represent a socialistic dilution of managerial freedom to manage. The second is that managers find that the union leaders enrolled in the seminar from other companies are surprisingly responsive to the concepts of industrial democracy illustrated in the seminar. When the seminar is first presented in a new region, union representatives may not be in attendance. In this case, managers enrolled in the program typically respond skeptically that "the union won't buy it." Thus having responsive union representatives in the seminar gives it a credibility usually not attainable solely through managerial testimony.

Having participated in, and determined the "safeness" of, the program for preserving company sovereignty, the next scheduled seminar will typically include management returnees and representatives from their bargaining unit(s). In no cases have union members rejected the theme of the seminar, and in most cases the union members have pushed for importing the concepts into the company in the form of an in-house workshop involving both management and labor.

In a few cases, union representatives have rejected management's invitation to participate in the public seminar. This rejection is typically a consequence of two factors—a climate of mistrust within the organization and the style in which the invitation was profferred. As noted earlier, altruistic motives are understandably perceived by adversaries as being ulterior. Under such conditions, a formal offer by "management" to finance "labor's" participation in a public seminar is automatically suspect. However, an informal (perhaps even unofficial) discussion between a member of management and a representative of labor might, on the basis of their mutual respect relationship, result in the union member's agreeing to an exploratory enrollment in the seminar. Even in a climate of mistrust, individuals from the "enemy camps" are sometimes thrown into mutual trust alliances on the basis of family ties or close-neighbor relationships or through association in religious, recreational, civic, or political activities.

Management must also be sensitive to the precarious political status of union leaders. Unlike managers who are appointed to their positions, union leaders are elected by their constituency. If a union election is coming up within six months, candidates for reelection seldom wish to jeopardize their status quo by making themselves vulnerable to opponents' allegations of being too friendly with management. On the other hand, managers and union leaders should be sensitive to groundswells of sentiment sometimes encountered among members of bargaining units who favor more union-management cooperation. Electioneering candidates for union offices in this case might welcome an opportunity to earn additional credentials through their involvement in the union-management seminar.

In considering a union's attitude toward the subject of collaboration, it is found that the local and parent union may have conflicting views. The local union's initiative in cooperating may be quashed by the representative from the union head office, particularly if the home office represents a more conservative or traditional philosophy. However, when the business representative is included in the change process from the beginning and is invited to participate in the seminar, this opposition is likely to be less restrictive and is sometimes manifested as, or converted to, active support. By and large, the union home office takes its cues from the local in terms of its role in intervention. If the local represents a trouble-free, stable membership, the home office is reluctant to take a stand which might alienate the membership. Sometimes the business representative takes a more positive and aggressive stand on the subject of collaboration than the local union. A timid local union in this case may receive encouragement and leadership from its headquarters' representatives.

A strong local union usually proves to be more of an asset to the organization than a union that is docile and compliant. Though a weak union may acquiesce to the idea of entering into collaborative effort, it may be psychologically unprepared to assume an active supportive role in participative practices. Union activists are often thwarted motivation seekers whose unfulfilled achievement motives tend to find expression in counterproductive or anticompany activities. This talent, converted to joint-stake pursuit of organizational objectives, can turn out to be one of the company's and union's greatest mutual assets.

Sometimes the threat of an impending crisis creates the opportunity to broach the subject of collaboration. The curtailment of business because of quality problems, unanticipated costs, waste, work interruptions, shrinking productivity, aggressive competition, product obsolescence, and economic recessions may precipitate threats to job security to which people willingly rally.

Finally, it should be noted that many people lead lives of quiet desperation in the workplace. Many have long ago despaired of having a meaningful and positive role in influencing the nature of their jobs and their work environment. The proffered new opportunity to use their minds, as well as their hands, represents a welcome respite from the oppressive world of monotony and petty rebellion. The spirit in which they enter the seminar is typically one of curiosity and skepticism. But at least it's more interesting and dignified to participate in a management seminar as a legitimate responsibility than it is to carry on in what is often a reactive or humdrum role in their everyday jobs.

Any of the foregoing factors may represent obstacles to or opportunities for getting members of management and labor to embark on a shared growth experience. Strategies are built on serendipitous circumstances within the organization, and the first step of the mission is to use whatever means are available to get management and union people to share a growth experience. The attitude with which they emerge from the seminar is, of course, a function of the relevance of this educational experience to their personal circumstances.

The Orientation Seminar

Participation in the one-day orientation seminar is an intrinsically interesting experience, away from the inhibiting influence of status symbols and other organizational constraints. It is a mind-stretching experience in which all can participate, where ideas stand on their own merit, without the intrusion of official authority and role limitations. For the union representative, the day is a positive stroke from the organization which says, "You are a creative person who can help your union and company consider new relationships."

"Family" groupings occur spontaneously in the seminar room. Union members from a common organization tend to form clusters—usually toward the back of the room. Managers from the same organization also tend to cluster, separately from their union members. So strong is this clannishness that nonsmokers will sit in the smoking section to be with their peers, or smokers will refrain from smoking in order to join peers in the nonsmoking section. This clustering usually carries over into the morning coffee break and lunch period.

Facial expressions of union people may reflect tenseness and cynicism or sometimes defensiveness, hostility, and feigned disinterest. In the beginning, they rarely speak up in the meeting, but may frequently whisper to each other during the seminar. However, if the conference leader succeeds in creating a climate of approval and is skillful in the use of overhead, relay, reverse, and directed questions, by lunch time open discussion begins to flourish. The lunch period tends to foster a socializing process that cuts across clusters as participants become engrossed in discussing issues surfaced during the morning.

Managers' faces and remarks also reflect a variety of attitudes. In the beginning some exhibit a reserved or skeptical wait-and-see posture. Most are pleased to find union people present and are openly curious to hear their viewpoints. A few tend to be solicitous or condescending toward union representatives; others may covertly express indignation to their peers and to the conference leader about this new encroachment on their territory. Accustomed to playing their cards close to their chest, they assert or hint darkly, "If you give them an inch, they'll take a mile." If they hear union members from other organizations expressing enlightened and positive viewpoints and if their organization has no union representatives in the seminar, they are inclined to believe, "Our union is different and totally incapable of taking a constructive position on anything!" Some express the viewpoint that union people say the right words in the seminar only because they are enjoying a day off with pay and a free lunch. Some union people *are* irresponsible, of course, but managers who give accurate descriptions of union dereliction ofter make inaccurate assumptions about the root cause of this behavior. Some managers have sponsored their union participation "on a wing and a prayer" as a last-ditch effort, with the fragile hope that some kind of magic might evolve from this experience. Some managers, of course, are sophisticated in theory of organizational behavior and are rationally seeking strategies for bridging the knowledge and social gap between management and labor.

The seminar content in no way places the blame for past or present conflict on either management or labor, but rather helps participants understand how conflict may be unintentionally precipitated by the actions of one or both parties. In this sense, the seminar is an experience in "mirror-holding" that enables participants to understand the cause-and-effect relationship of various types of behavior.

The topic outline for the public orientation seminar is the same as that for the in-house workshop (see pp. 95-104), minus the opportunity for participants to become comfortably acquainted with one another and to participate in work-group assignments, role playing, candid discussion, and the development of on-the-job implementation commitments (Exhibit 19).

The seminar is begun with a statement of the principles or assumptions on which union-management collaboration is based. These principles, listed in Exhibit 20, serve to establish the fact that the seminar is neither promanagement nor prolabor. Neither company nor union will be required to relinquish status. To the contrary, these principles define conditions of acceptance and respect for the union not usually received from management. At the same time, it attributes to the union an image of strength, responsibility, and democracy not always practiced by the union. Hence management representatives see defined in this list a set of conditions which require acceptance and support of the organizational charter by a responsible union, and the union members are assured of a legitimate role in the organization. Both parties recognize that these conditions do not presently exist, and both know that they can be realized only through joint commitment.

Seminar participants each receive a notebook containing materials related to the seminar content. Because articles and forms distributed during such seminars are often overlooked and forgotten by seminar participants, these handouts are reviewed at this time. Familiarity with this information also minimizes the requirement for note taking and thereby facilitates active participation during the day. The fact that some of these materials have been authored by union leaders is reassuring to union participants, who may be uneasy about the concept of union-management cooperation.

1. Statement of labor-relations principles
2. Review handout material
3. Principles of human motivation
   a) Hierarchy of needs
   b) Causes of productive and counterproductive behavior
   c) Jellybean theory and Christmas-turkey syndrome
   d) Work versus play
4. Changing values in society
   a) Obsolescence of two-class system
   b) Every employee a manager
   c) Adapting jobs to modern values
5. Communications
   a) Language of words—conversation, newspapers, bulletins, instructions, handbooks, letters, grapevine
   b) Language of action—leadership style, task forces, natural work groups, open door and open floor, problem solving, goal setting, grievance handling, listening, facial expressions, social gatherings
   c) Language of systems—attitude surveys, performance review, compensation, status symbols, career development, grievance procedure, collective bargaining, coffee bar, lunch room, work standards, signal bells
6. Interrupting the win-lose cycle
7. Media for joint effort
8. Media for joint stake
9. Life enrichment in the work place
10. Review of labor-relations principles

Exhibit 19 Orientation seminar outline.

1. Management accepts unionism and collective bargaining.
2. The union understands and accepts the operating charter.
3. Management considers a strong union an asset.
4. The union is strong, responsible, and democratic.
5. Management does not meddle in union affairs.
6. Management does not seek to undermine union allegiance.
7. Mutual trust exists between the two parties.
8. Neither party uses a legalistic approach to problem solving.
9. Conflicts are resolved through consultation and information sharing.
10. Conflicts are settled promptly, flexibly, and locally.
11. Negotiations are problem-centered, not abstractions.
12. Management and union share a common data base.
13. All members recognize their joint financial stake.

Exhibit 20 Guiding principles for company-union relationships.

Handout materials are not standardized, as they are continuously updated as new information becomes available. Following is a typical list of handouts for a one-day public seminar on union-management cooperation conducted during the writing of this book.

1. Roster of participants. The roster with job titles and organizational affiliations facilitates interpersonal interaction, particularly if participants wear identification tags during coffee breaks, lunch period, and seminar discussions.

2. "The Union and Improving the Quality of Work Life," Irving Bluestone (Vice President of the United Auto Workers international union), *Atlanta Economic Review*, No. 3, May-June 1974. A statement of joint commitment to the support of job enrichment by General Motors Corporation and the UAW.

3. "Who Are Your Motivated Workers?" M. Scott Myers, *Harvard Business Review,* January-February 1964. Conditions in the work place that motivate and dissatisfy employees.

4. "Every Employee a Manager," M. Scott Myers, *California Management Review,* Fall 1966. Conditions under which employees are managers of their own job rather than subservient followers of orders.

5. "Overcoming Union Opposition to Job Enrichment," M. Scott Myers, *Harvard Business Review*, May-June 1971. Strategies for breaking the win-lose cycle and for converting adversary into collaborative relationships between company and union.

6. "Doing Away with the Factory Blues," Donald N. Sobel, *Harvard Business review*, October-November 1975. How the Eaton Corporation is removing the status differential between office and factory employees and developing a climate of trust and commitment in the organization.

7. "From Paternalism to Industrial Statesmanship," Chapter 8 in Robert Blake and Jane Mouton, *Corporate Excellence Through Grid Organizational Development*, Houston: Gulf, 1968, pp. 175-200. A step-by-step description of a constructive confrontation between local union leaders and managers in a major Canadian supermarket-department store chain, which led to a collaborative pursuit of organizational goals.

8. "Worker Participation: Contrasts in Three Countries," Nancy Foy and Herman Gadon, *Harvard Business Review*, May-June 1976. A comparison of labor relations practices in the United States, England, and Sweden in terms of scope, philosophy, and techniques of participation.

9. "Profit Sharing—One of the New Breed of Total Systems Incentives," Bert L. Metzger, *Atlanta Economic Review,* May-June 1974. Profit sharing, as one of a growing family of sharing plans, which also include Scanlon plans, Rucker plans, and Employee Stock Ownership Plans (ESOP), is described in terms of its psychological and economic impact on the organization.

10. "The Scanlon Plan Has Proved Itself," Frederick G. Lesieur and Elbridge S. Puckett, *Harvard Business Review,* September-October

1969. A review of three companies that have operated for many years under Scanlon plans.

11. "Rucker Plan of Group Incentives," Robert C. Scott, *The Encyclopedia of Management*, 2d ed., New York: Van Nostrand Reinhold, 1973. A detailed description of a sharing plan based on employee collaboration for improving "valued added."

12. "A Piece of the Action," *Forbes*, May 1, 1975. A discussion of Kelso's Employee Stock Ownership Plan for granting employees a second income through stock ownership in the organization. The ESOP offers tax advantage to the organization and stimulates a joint financial stake among its members.

13. "How Attitude Surveys Can Help You Manage," M. Scott Myers, multilith. The employee attitude survey as a vehicle for involving people at all organizational levels in the solution of problems in the work place, thereby evoking creative and responsible behavior.

14. "TI Improvement Survey," a 95-item survey form used by Texas Instruments, Incorporated, in its periodic attitude surveys.

15. "Transactional Analysis Summary," Susan S. Myers, multilith. A two-page illustration and discussion of transactions and strokes.

16. Group psychological positions chart. A one-page work sheet to enable participants to understand union-management approaches to problem solving in terms of the TA four basic positions.

17. Communication media. A one-page listing of approximately 70 media or systems which shape the attitudes of people in the work place.

18. "Participative Management at Work," John F. Donnelly, *Harvard Business Review,* January-February 1977. John Donnelly, president of Donnelly Mirrors, is interviewed by David W. Ewing and Pamela Banks of the HBR staff regarding the evolution and practice of industrial democracy at Donnelly Mirrors.

Content of Orientation Seminar

Principles of motivation are presented in terms of both theory and applications. Maslow's hierarchy of needs is presented and translated into the media of the organization, as illustrated in Exhibit 1. It is shown that the thwarting of motivation needs leads to counterproductive or irrelevant use of talent and to excessive preoccupation with maintenance needs. The paternalistic attempt to motivate people with wages, hours, and working conditions is defined as the jellybean strategy, as shown in Exhibit 15. Jelly beans are defined as unearned rewards, such as Christmas turkeys or free coffee, which come to be expected whether the business can afford it or not. Bowling, as a recreational pursuit, is analyzed to illustrate the characteristics of meaningful and meaningless activity.

The changing values of society are explained in terms of conditions influencing the management-labor dichotomy. Money and knowledge, once the determinants of upper- or lower-class identity, are now being equalized so that blue-collar workers are essentially as well paid and as well informed as white-collar employees.

The worker's job is compared with the manager's job to explain the contrasting levels of motivation between managers and workers. Strategies are presented for enriching workers' jobs to include the planning and controlling functions which parallel managers' jobs. A manager is defined as any person who manages his or her own job.

Job enrichment is described, not as a narrowly oriented manipulative process, but as a process in which the job incumbent takes an active part. Job incumbents may assist in restructuring their own jobs; they may take the initiative in bidding on other jobs or swapping jobs with each other. They may have an active role in analyzing attitude survey results and prescribing remedies and in general have a broader participative role in influencing the climate of the workplace.

Communications is presented in terms of transactional analysis concepts and the media for communicating as the languages of words, actions, and systems. Whether the media be conversation (words), supervisory style (actions), or performance reviews (systems), examples are given to illustrate the contrasting impact of Parent-Child and Adult-Adult transactions. The adversary consequences of "We're OK, they're not OK" are shown to lead to company-union win-lose conflict, whereas the "We're OK, they're OK" orientation can lead to consensus and collaboration. Exhibit 21 is a framework with adjectives or descriptors provided by union and management participants in an in-house workshop.

Techniques for interrupting the company-union win-lose relationship include crisis sharing, negotiated collaboration, reorientation of organizational climate, and union involvement in management training. In all cases, the focus is on building mutual trust and putting both parties on a common data base.

While adversaries are learning to work together, the media for joint effort are usually restricted to processes not critically related to collective-bargaining issues. Examples of "safe" media include, but are not restricted to, attitude surveys, company newspaper, workplace layout, job design, recreational activities, health and safety, civic or community projects, and problem-solving efforts. As mutual trust develops and people become more comfortable in collaborative efforts, they may begin focusing on joint-stake issues such as productivity, cost effectiveness, and compensation policy.

The total one-day orientation seminar gradually leads to an understanding of the concept "life-enrichment in the workplace." The various components of the day-long seminar are shown to be mutually reinforcing and interdependent and to comprise a strategy for bringing synergy to the

	WE'RE OK, THEY'RE NOT OK	WE'RE NOT OK, THEY'RE OK	WE'RE NOT OK, THEY'RE NOT OK	WE'RE OK, THEY'RE OK
Adjectives that describe this group	Aggressive Domineering Condescending Paternalistic Exclusive Selfish Arrogant Independent Opportunistic Arbitrary	Defensive Subservient Ingratiating Dependent Weak Withdrawn Low profile Unassuming Hopeful Evasive	Unpredictable Irresponsible Ineffective Anarchistic Negative Unstable Uncommitted Ungrateful Quarrelsome Disrespectful	Effective Respectful Trustworthy Approachable Friendly Cooperative Open-minded Helpful Positive Resilient
Typical feelings of group members	Arrogance Confidence Cockiness Security Conceit Smugness Solidarity Superiority Impatience Holier than thou	Insecurity Inferiority Fear Inadequacy Incompetence Powerlessness Helplessness Envy Guilt Suspicion	Futility Despondence Apathy Despair Guilt Fear Anger Frustration Suspicion Resignation	Mutual Respect Optimism Enthusiasm Commitment Compatibility Confidence Unity Humility Sociability Solidarity
This group's approach to handling conflict	Parent-Child Domination Finger pointing Unyielding Manipulation Bluffing Kill with kindness Unilateral action Win-lose One-upman-ship	Child-Parent Avoidance Get away from Soliciting sympathy Begging Prayer Compromise Surrendering Submission Arbitration	Child-Child Arbitration Anarchy Run away from Retaliation Finger pointing Fatalism Abandonment May day! Arbitration	Adult-Adult Collaboration Confrontation Working through Cooperation Mutual trust Levelling Consensus Live and let live Listening

Exhibit 21 Group psychological-positions chart.

workplace. Finally, in closing the seminar, the principles governing company-union relationships used to open the seminar (Exhibit 20) are once again reviewed and subjected to further discussion. This list now seems more credible and less utopian in the light of the day's experience.

THE IN-HOUSE WORKSHOP

The in-house workshop is usually a three-day elaboration of the one-day orientation seminar. But unlike the one-day seminar, which is largely information sharing, the workshop also includes prereading assignments and involvement opportunities for interpersonal skill and attitude development.

It is tailored to the circumstances of the organization and ideally involves equal numbers of nonunion and union personnel. The nonunion segment may include supervisory, administrative, professional, and office personnel. It is essential that the chief executive officer of the unit and other top-level managers be included in the workshop, particularly those having line relationships with bargaining unit people. If the organization involved in the workshop is a plant or department of a larger corporate or public entity, the nonunion segment may include one or more members from the corporate or head-office staff. The union segment typically involves local union officers, shop stewards, committeepeople, and other members of the bargaining unit as chosen by the local union leaders and/or suggested by company management. However, the local union leaders should have a key role in determining who from the bargaining unit should attend, including business managers and other union head-office representatives.

As union-management workshops are usually restricted to 40 participants, each group can enroll up to 20 participants. If broader participation is desired, two or more consecutive workshops may be necessary. Although it may be desirable for every member of the organization to experience the three-day workshop, logistics and budgetary constraints may not permit such broad coverage. A workable compromise is to follow up the three-day workshops with one-day orientation seminars to involve all persons not included in the workshops. These orientation seminars may accommodate more than 100 persons each. Hence it is necessary for the company and union to collaborate in identifying the individuals in each group who are to experience the full workshops and those who are to participate in the one-day orientation seminars immediately following the workshops.

Though the expense of organizing and conducting these in-house workshops and seminars is usually borne by the company, this fact is not to be used as justification for company domination of the change process. The budget allotted for this program is to be created in the spirit of an investment to be managed by and for both parties in pursuit of mutual objectives. Hence members of both parties function as peers throughout the workshop within jointly accepted constraints established by the company charter, union by-laws, customer commitments, legal parameters, budgetary guidelines, and the ground rules for an effective team.

When the workshops have been scheduled to the mutual satisfaction of both parties, prework is assigned. This is usually done by distributing materials as mail-outs from the personnel department. However, if distribution of materials through company channels might cause it to be perceived by the union as management domination, consideration should be given to evoking union initiative and assistance in distributing materials.

Prework usually consists of reading assignments dealing with principles of motivation, leadership styles, interpersonal relationships, communications, organizational climate, and teamwork. Three or four articles from the following list are typical prework assignments:

"In Defense of Theory Y," Edgar Schein

"Who Are Your Motivated Workers?" Scott Myers

"Every Employee a Manager," Scott Myers

"Doing Away with the Factory Blues," Don Scobel

"Participative Management at Work," John Donnelly

Each article is accompanied by a questionnaire, or "learning instrument," to be completed by each individual after reading each article. The articles and completed questionnaires are to be used during the seminar as a basis for developing consensus within union-management subgroups. In addition, of course, completion of the prework enables the workshop leaders to begin from a higher plateau of sophistication and thereby increase the amount of learning which takes place during the three-day time span.

The in-house workshop is conducted in a setting where participants need not feel uncomfortable. A hotel or other off-site location is preferred to on-site facilities to escape the role associations and constraints which tend to characterize the workplace. For example, the use of the board room and executive dining facilities for the workshop creates inescapable reminders to the union members of their status differential, which may cause them to feel pressure to acquiesce to these unnatural, overwhelming, and seemingly condescending overtures by management. The on-site workshop also has the disadvantage of interruptions for phone calls, signatures, and emergencies, which can disrupt the delicate balance of participative effort. By the same token, the workshop setting should not be perceived by the management elite as a slumming experience. Hence the more neutral setting of a motel, school room, church facility, or public building is more likely to escape the restrictive and inhibitive status symbols of the workplace. The ideal setting is neither too luxurious nor too spartan, but is chosen with a thoughtful regard to the participants in terms of comfortable facilities, enjoyable meals and refreshments, and high-quality learning resources.

The workshop is initiated by making introductions, when necessary, and by establishing the ground rules in terms of content, procedures, and purpose of the program. The seminar leader(s) establishes his or her neutral role as a change agent for human effectiveness—being neither "promanagement" or "prolabor" nor "antimanagement" or "antilabor." At the outset, the workshop leader presents and encourages discussion of the assumptions underlying the labor relations principles enumerated in Exhibit 20.

An important ground rule to establish at this point is that neither managers nor labor representatives will invoke their official authority during the course of the workshop in any way that would inhibit or restrict the thinking or behavior of the program participants. For example, before this rule was established, a business manager for a national union once intervened to prevent a shop steward from role playing the discussion of excessive absenteeism, on the basis that this was a management rather than a union concern.

In other words, the workshop participants are to act as though they are disengaged from their traditional organizational roles and until the afternoon of the last day of the workshop are taking a detached, but objective and active, role in a personal and professional learning process, to the outcome of which they are not expected or asked to declare advanced commitment. It is made clear that commitments are deferred until the afternoon of the third day.

Unlike the one-day orientation seminar, which is primarily lecture and question-and-answer, the three-day workshop is structured around seven processes:

1. Prework
2. Lecture
3. Question-and-answer
4. Open discussion
5. Social interaction
6. Subgroup activity
7. Strategy building.

Lectures are illustrated with visual aids and are conducted in an informal style which invites questions and comments. Lecture topics are supplementary to the prework topics and include all of the items listed in the orientation seminar outline (Exhibit 19), plus information unique to the organization. Company-related information may include production data, market conditions, competitor status, balance sheet criteria, and any other data relevant to the understanding of organizational effectiveness.

Questions and answers are important pump-primers and useful in developing widely shared interest in the lecture topics. The skillful conference leader overcomes the natural reticence of such groups through the use of overhead, directed, relay, and reverse questions and through the communication principles and techniques of transactional analysis. The questions posed by the participants, when appropriately redirected back to the group, often serve as a catalyst to open discussion. The conference leader's role in such discussions is largely that of a process consultant who helps the participants understand what they are doing to one another, helps keep the discussion on track, helps them avoid or to overcome polarizations, and encourages balanced participation. In the language of transactional analysis, the conference leader helps them to use their Adult to understand the counterproductive entrapments caused by their Parent tapes and sometimes by their Child personality components.

Social interaction is fostered by shared assignments and the appropriate use of humor during the meetings and through informality during coffee breaks and lunch periods. These socializing opportunities help overcome the exclusive clustering of union and management personnel normally observed at the opening session of the workshop. Prejudice is essentially a collection of Parent tapes. Therefore, the missionary zeal of adversaries, particularly observable among many union leaders, is characteristically a Parent type of orientation devoid of the humor and creativity of the Child personality component. The ability to activate the Child in the constructive expression of humor and creativity is an important step in unfreezing the initial rigid adversary posture and in developing empathy between the two parties.

The prework assignment provides a basis for subgroup activity which brings adversaries together for the purpose of reaching consensus. In a 30-person workshop equally represented by management and union, for example, the participants might be subdivided into five subgroups, each containing three management and three union representatives. Though the purpose of the prework and subgroup activity is to expedite the learning process, it has a more important by-product of creating a shared experience and providing a "safe" medium for developing consensus. Benign as this collaborative experience may appear on the surface, it represents a significant departure from the Parent tapes which typically orient the two parties to automatically oppose any position taken by the other. Thus the reprogramming of Parent tapes is begun subtly and gradually through a shared learning experience.

Subgroup activity is also focused on role-playing activity. Each of the subgroups is given assignments to role play the handling of conflict situations. These conflict situations themselves may have been defined through joint union-management group effort. Each group is asked to role play a problem situation related to job effectiveness, such as low-quality workmanship, chronic tardiness, abuse of sick leave, violation of safety standards, or interpersonal conflict. For example, one group of six will work together in developing three scripts for interacting with a person who is chronically tardy. Two persons will role play a Critical Parent-Child approach to handling the problem, two others will role play a Protective Parent-Child encounter, and two others will role play an Adult-Adult relationship. In addition to developing interpersonal skills, these situations often provide a source of fun and amusement, particularly when the management and union representatives play-act reversed roles. In these role reversals, union members will sometimes lampoon the presumed authoritarianism of the manager, and the managers in turn will exaggerate the alleged irresponsibility or stubborness of the union member.

Each role-play demonstration is followed by a feedback critique led by the conference leader. For persons steeped in the Parent-Child tradition, it is unnatural and difficult to role play a credible Adult-Adult encounter. Such attempts often come through as Protective Parent or as a stiff and unnatural Adult. The participants often remark that it is easier and more fun to role play the Parent-Child relationships. This observation provides a basis for understanding the importance of being natural in the encounter and the desirability of mixing appropriate humor (Child) with the Adult message, if indeed the use of humor is an authentic component of the individual's personal style. Time permitting, some of the stiff and unnatural Adult-Adult demonstrations may be reenacted.

By the middle of the third day, the subgroups have experienced seven or eight shared learning experiences requiring collaborative efforts. In addition, through the lectures and discussions, they now share a common data base related to personal and organizational effectiveness. They have jointly acquired a common language, which is a partial basis for solidarity, much as the secret password is a symbol of common membership in fraternal organizations. Moreover, these experiences have not undermined or weakened the charter of either. Indeed, their shared experience is a basis for giving credibility to the labor relations principles listed in Exhibit 20.

During the afternoon of the third day, the subgroups direct their efforts to strategy development—the application of principles and techniques learned in the workshop. This is the stage where the participants begin using their new relationships developed in the "protected" environment of the workshop for the purpose of developing strategies which can be applied in the real world of the workplace.

The subgroups are given an assignment consisting of a four-part question:

"In the light of the context of this three-day workshop:

1. What are we doing now in support of these principles?

2. What new things might we begin doing?

3. What are we doing now that we should modify or discontinue?

4. What are our major obstacles?"

They are given one hour to brainstorm answers to these four questions and are asked to designate a time-keeper to see that they spend no more than 15 minutes on each of the four parts of the question. They are instructed to use a democratic process to select a person in each subgroup who will record the answers to these four questions and report back to the general session.

Because this last subgroup assignment focuses on important job issues and relationships, it is the most animated part of the workshop. No guidelines other than "democratic process" are given for selecting spokespersons to report recommendations to the general session. In practice, it is rather evenly balanced between management and union, with the latter tending to represent a slight majority.

Reports may be written on flip charts, transparency acetates, or simply on note pads. These reports are displayed and/or read and explained to the total session by the selected spokespersons. Questions for clarification are encouraged during reports, but questions of controversy are held until all reports are completed. Each report typically requires five to ten minutes. Overlap commonly exists among the several reports; however, each report also typically contains unique and creative suggestions. To the surprise of many, the quality and content of the reports made by union members do not differ from the reports made by managers.

Exhibit 22 lists topics that typically appear on subgroup reports. After all reports are completed, a plan is developed to consolidate them into a master report. Ideally, this consolidation takes place immediately, usually through the efforts of a volunteer task force from the workshop participants. The personnel manager or training director tends to volunteer or be selected to head up such a task force; however, the resulting action plan is more likely to be implemented under the guidance of a line manager. The consolidated report is to go to each workshop participant and to the chief executive officer. If the chief executive officer was not a participant in the workshop, his or her presence during the final reporting session is desirable to orient him or her to the spirit and rationale of the recommendations.

Immediate attention is directed to the listed "obstacles," as some of these can have an immediate neutralizing impact on the commitments developed by the workshop participants. For example, the item "union member suspicions" refers to union leaders' fears that their membership will accuse them of playing "footsie" with management. Some of them had already heard remarks to that effect when they enrolled in, or during the course of, the workshop. Another item, "opposition from union headquarters," reflects their fear of intervention by the business manager or other higher-ups in the union hierarchy.

The value of a strong and democratic local union cannot be stressed enough. A large manufacturing company in Ohio encountered opposition from the international union when it attempted to install Scanlon plans in its plants. However, by going directly to the local union membership, the company mustered the necessary support to override the international union's opposition and subsequently installed the Scanlon plan in 14 plants.

Another obstacle, "management inertia," becomes a challenge to invalidate that allegation. It is not necessary, or even realistic, to attempt to implement all recommendations immediately. But it is important, and feasible, to act immediately in consolidating the list of recommendations and within two weeks begin establishing priorities and action plans which can involve and be shared with the participants of the workshop and orientation seminars.

Though personnel or other staff functions may consolidate the various subgroup reports into a master list to serve as the basis for action plans,

1. *Things we are doing now in support of these concepts:*
   Some employees planning their own work
   Tuition-refund program
   Merit pay for salaried people
   Union-management safety committee
   Clean work environment
   Open-door policy
   Department meetings
   Paid suggestion plan
   Promotion from within
   Job posting for union employees
   Credit union
   Limited job rotation

2. *New things to begin:*
   All people involved in Plan-Do-Control
   Introduce work-simplification program
   Begin using attitude surveys
   Establish merit pay for high performers
   Introduce Scanlon plan
   Let present employees interview job candidates
   More professional-development programs for workers
   Eliminate reserved parking lots based only on rank
   Let people inspect their own work where feasible
   Eliminate time clocks and other status symbols
   Adult performance-review system
   Flex-time where feasible
   Employee-managed newspaper

3. *Things to modify or discontinue:*
   Abolish piece-work incentive system
   Give more weight to merit and less to seniority
   Extend job posting to office and management jobs
   Safety committee have rotating chairpersons
   Safety committee meet with OSHA reps and file reports
   Make paid suggestion plan part of Scanlon plan
   Have only one color for hard hats
   Supplement open door with open-floor policy
   More opportunities for job rotation—including across crafts
   Automatic pay increases for all
   Let employees plan company picnic

4. *Major obstacles:*
   Theory X values—both management and union
   Possible opposition from union headquarters
   Budgets and manpower restrictions
   Constraints imposed by corporate headquarters
   Union member suspicion
   Not enough feedback
   Resistance to change
   Excessive paperwork
   Loss of union leadership through promotions

Exhibit 22 Union-management workshop subgroup report.

establishing priorities and carrying out action plans are line functions to be initiated through the joint involvement of chief executives and key union leaders. When action plans become "personnel programs," they tend to suffer from downgraded priority, whereby they are pushed aside in deference to other line problems. In short, the likelihood of genuine union-company collaboration occurring and persevering is directly a function of the extent to which these efforts are integrated into mainstream operations.

Following a public orientation seminar or an in-house workshop, the participants, both management and union, are usually enthusiastic about applying these concepts in the workplace. Participants from the public seminar wish to follow up with an in-house workshop, and in-house workshop graduates are impatient to get on with their commitments. However, for most participants this enthusiasm wanes quickly unless immediate steps are taken to reinforce it. In addition, resolutions may be undermined by the attitudes of the members of the bargaining unit who did not participate in the program. Many of the nonparticipants view collaboration with management in any form with suspicion, as an act of disloyalty or capitulation. Also, union business managers and other representatives of regional or national union offices may feel threatened by strategy changes which did not involve them. They may view these changed relationships as a manipulative ploy by management to weaken the role of unions. Or, they may see the participation of the local union with management as a process which could create a breach between the international union and its locals. Hence the would-be collaborators may find themselves subjected to various direct or subtle pressures to return to their traditional adversary approach.

The problem is not all created by the union, of course. Managers also have second thoughts upon returning to their workplace, particularly traditionally oriented persons who see participation with the union as a form of capitulation and a threat to their managerial prerogatives. Managers who were not included in the workshop may decry out of ignorance the dangers of permissiveness and creeping socialism. But if the chief executive officer has participated in the seminar and has emerged as an active supporter of the new strategy, backsliding is less likely to occur, particularly if the CEO has activated a number of immediate follow-up action programs. However, if only members of middle and lower management have participated, the responsibility for initiating what appears to be a radically new labor relations philosophy is more than most conservative career-oriented managers are willing to assume.

The primary mission of the workshop, of course, is to initiate a lasting process for establishing management and labor on a common data base, with a common mission, in a climate of mutual trust. This process is begun in the workshop through involvement with "safe" topics, such as principles of motivation, hierarchy of needs, human relations, communications, and problem-solving techniques. Under this temporary condition of mutual trust and enthusiasm resulting from shared experience in the workshop, participants commit themselves to supporting new approaches and to modifying or discontinuing certain established practices. In the climate of the classroom, these commitments seem credible.

Back on the job, after the workshop, participants may continue in this collaborative mode, but only if dealing with "safe" subjects not directly associated with the pivotal issues of collective bargaining. These nonthreatening subjects might include the company newspaper, recreational activities, problem-solving efforts, and employee orientation programs. Extended involvement in these safe media achieves two purposes. One, it represents a natural extension of the workshop and as such tends to perpetuate and reinforce feelings of mutual trust among the participants. Second, these systems develop mutual proprietary interest in goals and processes which contribute at least indirectly to organizational effectiveness. After a year or more of joint involvement in mutually chosen projects, the former adversaries gradually find themselves drawn naturally and mutually into areas which earlier would have been too delicate for joint handling, such as job descriptions, job evaluation, interfunctional responsibilities, the role of seniority, merit pay, sharing plans, and conflict resolution.

Media for joint effort are usually determined serendipitously by the opportunities unique to each organization and to the perceptions of its members. Hence no standard list can be prescribed for application in all organizations.

ATTITUDE SURVEYS

One exception to this generalization is the attitude survey, provided, of course, it is appropriately administered. The attitude survey is not only universally applicable, but, more important, it also serves as a medium for identifying other opportunities for organizational improvement through joint effort. Its universality stems from the fact that it is responsive to the attitudes and values of the survey participants. Because collaboration is a state of mind, or attitude, the survey, which serves to measure, redirect, and modify attitudes, is uniquely appropriate as a vehicle for engendering participation. Undertaken as a joint effort by management and labor, surveys serve both as an educational process in systems development and as a process for directing the efforts of all members of the organization toward organizational improvements. Though other media for collaboration may also serve important roles, it will be shown that the attitude survey is the system which unites most other media into a cohesive framework.

Traditionally, attitude surveys are initiated by upper management, with little or no involvement of the vast majority of the population whose attitudes are to be measured. Worse yet, attitude surveys are sometimes conducted by personnel functions or outside consultants, with little or no participation by line management. In the first instance, respondents seldom understand the purpose of the survey and tend to perceive it as a management tool, initiated for some ulterior or manipulative purpose. In the second case, the survey may be perceived as a personnel project, spearheaded by "missionaries for participation," not intergrated into mainstream pursuits of organizational effectiveness. Thus action programs prescribed through the survey may lack support of the chief decision makers of the organization.

The attitude survey offers four opportunities for participation: (1) the design of the survey instrument, (2) the completion of the survey form, (3) the analysis of survey results, and (4) the development of remedial action programs. The most benign of these is the second, the completion of the survey form. Yet it is the only opportunity offered in most organizations.

However, the completion of the survey has more meaning when experienced as part of the total four-step process. Conversely, the completion of the survey form in the absence of the other three processes can render it meaningless or even frustrating to respondents who wonder about the purpose and results of the survey. Indeed, it may be argued that partial participation can be more harmful than helpful if it results in misunderstanding or unfulfilled expectations.

In the impoverished circumstances of meaningless and unchallenging work, any interruption in the monotonous routine is welcomed. The completion of a survey form in such circumstances at least provides an opportunity to escape the job for a half hour and represents a new topic to enliven the grapevine. However, this limited participation is a form of tokenism, which at best offers a brief respite from monotony and at worst becomes a vehicle for the selective, unilateral, and paternalistic implementation of "remedial actions" by management.

Though the completion of the survey form is a form of participation, it is relatively ineffectual compared to the opportunity afforded by the feedback process. Unfortunately, survey results are usually subjected to guarded and defensive analysis and are ultimately issued as whitewashed reports in the company newspaper. Needless to say, such an approach in the unionized organization would incur the resentment, if not the opposition, of the union. In one organization, for instance, a personnel director had developed and printed a survey form based on the content of other company surveys and what he and other top-management people thought to be relevant questions for their organization. He had the forms printed and somewhat as an afterthought approached a local union representative and said to him, "We are contemplating administering this attitude survey." Without looking at the survey form the union representative retorted, "If you do, we'll close you down." The personnel director handed the questionnaire to the union representative and said, "How would you change it?" The union representative took the form, scanned it, and said, "I'll let you know tomorrow." He reviewed the form with fellow union officials and brought it back to the personnel director the next day with approximately six questions edited. He said, "OK. If you make these changes, we'll accept it." Actually, the editorial changes were minor and easily incorporated into the survey. Through only this limited amount of participation by the union, the company avoided what could have become a major conflict issue.

However, such limited involvement of the union is only tokenism and will not yield the benefits of an authentic collaborative effort. An authentic participative approach evokes the joint efforts of company-union task forces, made up from all levels and functions of the organization, in developing the purpose and concept of the attitude survey, the content of the survey form, the administration procedure, the analysis of survey results, and the implementation of resultant action programs.

Organization Development Through Attitude Surveys

The following model of the attitude survey as a medium for union-management collaboration is a composite of actual applications in both union and nonunion organizations. Applications in union and nonunion situations are identical in that both cases involve task forces from all levels and functions of the organization. However, members of a nonunion organization relate their efforts to a common cause under a common charter, whereas members of the unionized work force pursue the same common cause within constraints which protect the realms of mutual independence between company and union. The model, as described herein, presumes the existence of one or more labor unions.

As a consequence of an in-house workshop, both company and union agree to undertake a companywide attitude survey as a joint effort. Both top management and union officials are involved in a discussion that leads to consensus regarding the purpose, procedure, and schedule for the survey. Through regularly scheduled departmental meetings, each department head brings up the subject to all members of his or her department, saying, in effect, "The company and union have agreed in principle to the idea of an attitude survey as a means of identifying and dealing with problems and for measuring and reinforcing the good features of the organization. Because you are the persons best acquainted with the organization, your help is needed to select questions for the survey." The department head asks each individual, working independently or in small groups, to write up to ten questions that he or she would like to see included in the survey. To facilitate the creative process, all individuals are given a one-page copy and description of Exhibit 1 to use as a framework for thinking of questions. They are advised to consider each of the six "maintenance" and four "motivation" categories as a guide for writing the questions. In one organization of 1200 members, approximately 2000 questions were generated. These questions were collated by subject matter and edited by a companywide joint task force under the guidance of the personnel department.

This review and consolidation process weeds out redundancies and usually results in a reduction of items to about ten percent of the original list. This shortened list of questions is duplicated as a preliminary form for distribution to all individuals, whose assistance is sought for the purpose of detecting omissions, removing ambiguities, and establishing a priority for shortening the questionnaire to 100 or fewer items.

In the organization noted above, the list of 2000 questions was reduced to 200 in the preliminary screening process and to 150 through the involvement of all employees during department meetings. Though an attempt was made to reduce the items to 100, a trial administration to 30 employees showed that the 150 items were not too time-consuming or tedious. However, the educational level and language skills of people in this organization were above average, and in most organizations the 100-item limit is a sound guideline.

The final form is administered to all members of the organization during regular working hours. To minimize production interruptions, employees may be convened in small groups throughout each shift. If working-hour interruptions are not permissible, overtime (with pay) may be used. Administration time seldom exceeds 30 minutes. Mailing questionnaires to the home or distributing questionnaires for completion on employee time, is not satisfactory, as it rarely yields more than a 60 percent return.

Questionnaires are usually administered by representatives of the personnel department in the cafeteria and conference rooms near work sites. Some managers choose to have questionnaires administered and analyzed by a neutral outsider (college professor or consultant), on the assumption that this neutrality will ensure greater candor. Although this may be true for the initial administration, the experience of participating in an anonymous company-administered survey will do much to establish a climate of trust, particularly if the administration guidelines are jointly established by company and union.

Respondents from various organizational levels may be convened for administering the questionnaire, provided supervisors and union stewards do not sit next to respondents under their jurisdiction. Slotted boxes are provided at room exits for depositing completed questionnaires, thereby providing further assurance of anonymity. Moreover, administration instructions should specify that participation is voluntary and that any person not wishing to complete the form can simply drop the blank form in the box upon leaving, with the assurance that nonrespondents are also anonymous. In practice, uncompleted questionnaires are seldom received, although single items are occasionally omitted intentionally or through oversight. The conscientious responses obtained through such questionnaires are undoubtedly a function of the proprietary interest in the survey resulting from the respondents' involvement in developing it.

Completed survey forms are forwarded to data processing for keypunching. Keypunch operators are instructed to obliterate signatures or any unsolicited identifying information, on the assumption that departures from complete anonymity could ultimately inhibit candor and undermine survey validity.

Survey results are printed in profile from by attitude category and individual item, as shown in Exhibits 23 and 24, respectively. Separate

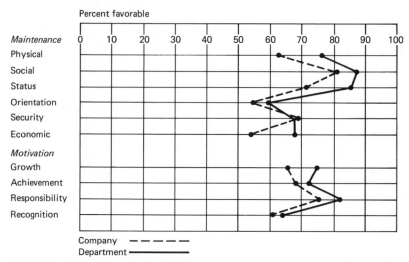

Exhibit 23 Improvement survey profile (maintenance-motivation categories).

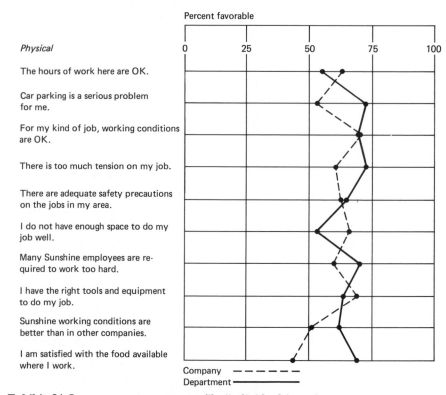

Exhibit 24 Improvement survey profile (individual items).

profiles are shown for the company and each department. Each department head receives a complete set for his or her department and the company in the form of transparencies suitable for projection. Department heads report the results to all employees during department meetings, candidly projecting the profiles on a screen and inviting questions and comments. Comparisons are made between departmental and total organization profiles, and when surveys are administered periodically, trends may be identified and traced. Though the candid feedback of survey results to all members of the department is in itself an educational process, it is only a foundation for the more action-oriented diagnositc process which follows.

The next step is to organize task forces in each department to analyze survey results and formulate remedial actions. Task-force members may be nominated by peers, selected by lottery, or simply chosen through supervisory and union-leader judgment. One of the guiding constraints in selecting task forces is the capability of the department to maintain uninterrupted productivity while providing opportunities for the task forces to function. Task forces vary in size from two to twelve members, but five or six is usual.

Task forces are given a four-point mission: (1) to study survey results and identify what they believe to be problems or obstacles to organizational effectiveness; (2) to determine the causes of these problems; (3) to prescribe actions for dealing with these problems; and (4) to identify any conditions or areas which the survey show to be quite favorable and to explain why these favorable conditions exist. In answering the third question, task forces are asked to put themselves in their department head's shoes by asking themselves, "What specifically can we do to resolve these problems within the constraints imposed by budgets, laws, schedules, market conditions, quality standards, prices, and personnel availability?" The fourth question is included to put the total process in perspective. When the focus is placed exclusively on identifying and dealing with obstacles and problems, task forces tend to develop a negatively distorted impression of the organization. Thus question four tends to provide a more balanced perspective as well as to identify positive features in the organization to be reinforced and perpetuated.

Task forces are given free access to any information desired and are encouraged to consult their peers in carrying out their task-force assignments. Because group activities of this type are easily sidetracked and prolonged, the task-force mission is specifically limited to the four questions enumerated above and restricted to a prescribed time frame of two to four weeks.

In most organizations it cannot be assumed that task-force members are already skilled in participative methods. When task forces are formed, they are asked to designate a member of the group to serve as coordinator for scheduling and chairing meetings and for preparing the written report. Logistics usually do not permit the training of all members in group processes;

however, it is usually feasible to give special instructions to the group coordinators. A half-day orientation session on conference leadership techniques, transactional analysis, decision making, and the functioning of an effective task force, usually yields a high return on investment. The use of the Group Feedback Form (Exhibit 18) enables task-force members to assess and improve their own group effectiveness during their assignment.

Attitude-survey task forces, as described above, vary considerably in terms of number and duration of meetings required to complete their assignments. An average of five two-hour meetings over a three-week period is normal. The final report may be handwritten, but is usually typed by a member of the task force or through typing services arranged by the department head. The quality of the final report is usually a reflection of the task force's proprietary interest in the project, and in most cases the reports given to the department head are meticulously prepared.

Upon receiving the completed report from the task force, the department head shares it with other managers in the department. In some organizations the managerial group will outline a suggested action plan to be reviewed and discussed with the task force. In other cases managers and task-force members participate in joint working sessions to develop action plans. The latter approach is less likely to create or perpetuate adversary polarizations, particularly when mutually understood constraints rather than official authority are the basis for goal setting.

When a course of action is agreed on, the department head shares the action plan with the balance of the work force through the medium of the department meeting. Though department meetings are typically chaired by the department head, more candid and spontaneous discussion may result if task-force coordinator(s) make the presentation and lead the discussion. This is particularly true if coordinators include members of the bargaining unit. Feedback to the total department is in terms of: (1) results of the attitude surveys; (2) remedial actions already implemented or to be undertaken immediately; (3) actions to be deferred to some specific date; and (4) recommendations that could not be acted on and the reasons why not. The department meeting feedback report is, ideally, accomplished within six weeks of the administration of the questionnaire.

It should be noted that the attitude-survey procedure, as described above, is more than just a tool for identifying problems that need resolving or for "measuring the pulse" of the organization. More important, it is a system that unites people from throughout the organization in a democratic process of problem identification and resolution. Members involved in such a process acquire a new perspective in conflict resolution not oriented around the management-labor dichotomy or through the use of official management or union authority. Rather, the information sharing and the working through to consensus are but an extension or additional dimension of the concept "every employee a manager."

Sometimes in the problem-identification process, if union-management relationships are perceived by a task force as a major obstacle or if some issue of collective bargaining is identified as a problem, the joint company-union task force may institute ground rules that would set aside certain specific issues for separate consideration through the traditional bargaining process. For instance, in one organization the attitude survey was used approximately six weeks before collective bargaining to surface and deal with all issues peripheral to wages, benefits, and job security, which were reserved for collective bargaining. Thereby, the organization was able to go into collective bargaining unfettered by side issues, which tend to complicate and extend the bargaining process. More important, the attitudes of the bargainers were more candid and democratic as a result of the survey's role in dissipating hostilities.

In viewing the attitude survey in total perspective, it is a medium for modifying the climate of an organization: first, by identifying the various elements in the organization which have impact on the organization climate; and second, by involving all members of the organization in the change process. In the traditional organization, no matter how altruistic the management and union may be in bringing about changes, if the basis for the change is not understood, and particularly if management and union coexist in a condition of mutual distrust, there is little opportunity to implement a mutually desirable change process. The changes brought about through the attitude survey are not achieved through the use of official authority by either management or the union. Because the process is not threatening to either company or union, being a member of either is largely irrelevant. Relevancy stems from the joint involvement of concerned people in the improvement of organizational effectiveness.

Attitude changes resulting from the involvement process may be manifested in various ways. For example, one organization experienced a sustained 50 percent reduction in absenteeism, dating from the department meetings in which the employees began writing questions for the survey. In addition to serving as a medium for joint effort, the attitude survey also serves to spawn other media for joint effort. If, for example, the attitude survey indicates that people feel they are not getting enough information, joint effort may be directed toward improving communications.

COMPANY NEWSPAPER

The company newspaper is often referred to as the "management's mouthpiece" to reflect the proprietary control that management has over it and its role in providing selected information to its readers. To the extent that the company newspaper is identified with management, particularly in an adversary union-management relationship, union members are inclined to take a cynical view of its contents because of their mistrust of its publisher. It is this feeling of mistrust that often leads to the development of the union newspaper or, in some organizations, the underground newspaper.

A newspaper can be interesting, relevant, and credible if its readers have a major hand in producing it. A manufacturing company of 1200 employees in South Carolina has a newspaper published monthly by members of the work force. Members of the newspaper staff are all volunteers and include an editor, associate editor, printer, typist, and 27 reporters. The editor and associate editor are elected by the reporters and serve overlapping two-year terms. Approximately two-thirds of the volunteer staff is from the hourly paid work force and the balance is from the salaried staff. However, the editors have always been members of the hourly paid work force. All members of the staff perform their duties for the newspaper in addition to their regular jobs for which they were hired; except for the editor, part of whose pay comes from an overhead budget, staff members are not compensated separately for their volunteer services. The newspaper typically consists of 16 to 20 pages covering a wide spectrum of topics, including those usually found in a traditional company newspaper, such as company goals, product lines, productivity achievements, safety programs, promotions, organizational changes, holiday announcements, charity drives, pay, and benefits. In addition, it usually includes announcements of birth dates, births, marriages, social and recreational activities, union activities, special awards, new hires, and a variety of personal-interest items. The newspaper differs from the traditional company paper in four respects: (1) it is written entirely by employees who are not compensated for their volunteer efforts; (2) the news items carry the contributors' bylines; (3) the paper is totally uncensored by upper management; and (4) it is written is the language of its readers.

RECREATIONAL PROGRAMS

Recreational programs offer the unique opportunity for people who are polarized in the work force to get to know and respect one another through media untainted by politics and official authority. Hence it is possible for members of management and labor to be in bowling leagues, softball teams, tennis clubs, and many other activities for which company and union role identification is irrelevant. Care must be taken, of course, to avoid the intrusion of rank-oriented status symbols into the policies and practices governing recreational activities. For instance, one organization permitted management people to wear special jackets carrying the company emblem. However, the hourly employees were not allowed this same privilege, on the presumption that they were inclined to be less responsible and hence would convey a poor image of the organization. Fortunately, this barrier to solidarity was eliminated by a simple policy change which made all employees eligible to buy and wear the company emblem. The previous discriminatory policy had its roots in an earlier era when blue-collar workers were economically, intellectually, and psychologically less capable of, or willing to, support and represent the company.

Sometimes polarizations are unwittingly reinforced through competitive team sports such as baseball, basketball, and bowling when "management" teams compete with "labor" teams. Though these team alignments seem natural and friendly, they do reinforce polarization which may be less friendly in the workplace. Competition oriented around departmental or functional identities has the advantage of uniting workplace adversaries in recreational teamwork, thereby reducing management-labor animosities.

Another pitfall associated with recreational activities stems from a traditional management practice of dominating recreational programs by providing their budgets, facilities, and direction. Under these circumstances, recreational activities are perceived as management-owned. One company routinely sponsored an annual picnic, chose the location, provided the refreshments, and sent invitations to all members of the work force over the president's signature. Contests and prizes were arranged by management, and a speech was given by the president from a table in the center of the picnic grounds. Despite managerial good intentions, picnic attendance diminished annually until it involved less than half the work force.

The key to successful recreational activities is joint ownership in planning, financing, and administering these programs. The company that had previously arranged the company picnic and financed it through an annual donation of $7000 put the entire recreational program in the hands of a company task force made up of a proportional diagonal slice of the organization. The budget managed by the task force was derived from employee contributions and a percentage of the plant's vending machine receipts. The purpose of the recreational task force is to decide how best to manage the recreational budget and satisfy the greatest number in the work force. In one year, for example, instead of spending all of the money on a picnic, it apportioned the funds to a picnic, a spaghetti dinner, and a dinner-dance. Moreover, the proprietary attitude spawned by the joint task force resulted in wider participation from all levels and functions of the company. Incidentally, the portion of the budget derived from the vending machine receipts did much to reduce the use of slugs and to dissipate a long-standing grudge against vending machines which had previously been perceived as a management rip-off.

In summary, recreational programs are more successful in depolarizing a work force if they are not a union or management function, but rather are managed by a task force representing all levels and functions of the organization. Though initial investments in recreational facilities may be made by the company in the same spirit that educational assistance is supported, the day-to-day and long-term administration of recreational activities should be achieved through the initiative and support of their users.

One employee-managed recreational program offers employees the option of paying a blanket annual fee of $25 entitling them to unlimited memberships or a choice of single memberships at $5 each.

JOB EVALUATION

Employees not in a bargaining unit generally have their pay levels established on the basis of compensation surveys and job evaluation. In the bargaining unit, however, there may be little or no relationship between the wage levels bargained for and the results of compensation surveys or job evaluation. This is not necessarily because union people do not believe in surveys or job evaluation. In fact, unions do their own kind of survey by selectively comparing themselves with other wage earners in their community and industry. Unions' mistrust of job evaluation is more often a reflection of their attitude toward management. They cannot expect to endorse a technical process they do not understand, particularly if their adversaries are well armed with expertise on the subject.

The best way to make sure that people understand a job-evaluation system is to make them a part of it. It is not necessary, of course, for all members of the work force to be able to do job evaluations, but it is possible and worth the effort to involve representatives from all major functions and levels in the organization. Thus a wage and salary administrator, as chairperson, forms a task force from all levels and functions to participate in the installation or updating of a job-evaluation system. Though some task-force members are from the bargaining unit, the task force should not be established as a union-management process, but rather as a group chosen to integrate a wide variety of viewpoints. This permanent, part-time task force is briefed thoroughly on the job-evaluation procedure, philosophy, and the constraints within which it functions. For instance, task-force members need to be familiar with relevant labor laws, cost-of-living indices, comparative rates in the community and industry, and profitability forecasts.

Trial applications of the job-evaluation process on a few noncontroversial jobs will ensure understanding of the system and begin developing the team process. When the task force is ready to fulfill its mission, its initial effort is usually focused on the evaluation of "benchmark" jobs—typical multiple-occupancy jobs in all levels and functions. These benchmark jobs serve as standards against which other jobs are evaluated and slotted into the various job hierarchies. Although the main purpose of the job-evaluation process is to establish equitable wage and salary levels, an equally important function of the job-evaluation task force is to develop an understanding of the job-evaluation process at various levels and functions of the organization. This shop floor understanding is a natural tie-in to the grapevine. An explanation of the job-evaluation system by a peer is more likely to be solicited and is more credible than an explanation by an authority figure from management.

The existence of a task force for job-evaluation purposes does not negate the collective-bargaining process. It may still go on, but collective bargaining by members of a bargaining unit who understand job evaluation is much more likely to be responsibly keyed to the reality of the workplace.

TRAINING PROGRAMS

Most training activities are handled by training specialists headquarted in the personnel department. As a member of a staff function, the trainer often lacks credibility with the line manager. As a member of management, the trainer may be viewed by union people as a company propagandist. Hence a professionally competent trainer might be handicapped by the attitudes of his or her clients.

For this reason, as well as for logistical and economic constraints, trainers seek to integrate the training function with line responsibility. One of the most effective training programs at Texas Instruments during the 1960s was the Work Simplification training program conducted by 90 supervisors in an electronic assembly department of more than 3000 employees.

The same principle can be applied in unionized organizations when training effort impinges on what union members perceive as union business. For instance, managers in many organizations complain that union stewards do not have a uniform understanding of the terms of the union agreement. At the same time, shop stewards may complain that supervisors do not understand the terms of the agreement. Hence the problem is clearly pinpointed as one in which both supervisors and members of the bargaining unit need a more uniform understanding of the spirit and letter of the union contract. However, a training program initiated by management to train the people in the content of the bargaining agreement may lack acceptance by the union on the basis that trainers do not understand the agreement fully or present a management-oriented viewpoint. The problem may be solved by establishing a joint union-management training team whose job is to plan, organize, and administer an orientation session for supervisors and union stewards. Such an orientation session can, of course, be presented to any or all members of the work force. Controversies that arise within the context of this presentation can be resolved through the joint involvement of both parties.

Another example of this joint effort was illustrated in a wood-products company. When installing new equipment that would require operator training, members of the bargaining unit were asked to help select peers who could serve as training assistants in getting the equipment on line. Two persons from the bargaining unit were nominated and sent to another site 1200 miles away, where the same type of equipment was already in operation. While on this two-week work assignment, they received their regular base pay plus travel costs. Upon completion of this training assignment, they assumed a key role in training the operators in their own bargaining unit. This departure from standard practice was well received by those affected—particularly the ad hoc trainers who experienced an increased sense of responsibility and favorable recognition. Though this assignment was clearly outside the definitions imposed by union-approved job descriptions, the union did not object to such a departure from standard procedure when it was so clearly favored by the membership.

In another organization, volunteer members of the bargaining unit were made a part of the new-employee orientation program. Volunteers were trained by the personnel department to assume responsibility for instructing new employees on the guidelines of conduct in the company, work standards, and other aspects of new-employee orientation. This type of involvement is not initiated by unilateral decisions of management, of course, but as one of the consequences of joint union-management efforts which led to better utilization of human resources in all parts of the organization.

PROBLEM-SOLVING TASK FORCES

In most polarized organizations, productivity is management's concern—not labor's. Worse yet, breakdowns that result in paid downtime may be a cause for rejoicing by the equipment operators. Moreover, engineers and equipment repairers tend to underrate the importance of the operator's attitude in operating and maintaining the equipment or his or her talent for designing and repairing it. Attitudes and talents not constructively harnessed find expression, of course, in counterproductive behavior. The malfunctioning of a foundry molding process and a brewery bottling machine was, in each case, mistakenly diagnosed and futilely treated as a technical problem. When correctly diagnosed and treated as a human problem, less time was devoted to repair, and further breakdowns were minimized.

The problem-solving, goal-setting process described in Chapter 2, whether it involves a natural work group or an ad hoc task force, is the most natural and potentially most effective method for putting all members on a common data base. It is a process that reorients the worker's self-image from that of a person who works with his or her hands to that of a person who is also valued for his or her ability to contribute with the mind. Goal-oriented task forces that cut across various levels and functions of the organization can gradually depolarize people away from the traditional management-labor gap. Hence the task force is not to be set up as a management-labor task force engaged in a new labor relations experiment, but rather as a group of concerned individuals pooling their talents in the pursuit of a common goal. The problem-solving task force is comprised initially of people who are closest to the system and most likely to be familiar with the causes of, and solutions to, the problem. The initial task force may have an understandable proprietary interest in the mission and should be consulted when inviting participants from other levels and functions into the group.

Task forces may ultimately function with little regard for organizational relationships and sometimes reach outside the organization to include customers, suppliers, or members of regulatory agencies. To the extent possible, task forces should convene in natural settings; for instance, if the task force includes people with soiled shoes or coveralls from the machine shop or foundry, they may not feel natural sitting in a carpeted board room. Problem-solving task forces are not usually established as permanent committees, but rather as ad hoc goal-oriented groups of individuals selected because of their potential influence in dealing with a specific problem. When the problem is solved, the task force is disbanded to be regrouped with the same, or preferably different, members when the next problem arises. The use of task forces is not focused on labor-management relations, but on the un-self-conscious process of making the organization function.

Chapter 6

Toward
Industrial Democracy

The foregoing discussion of processes and techniques for interrupting the win-lose cycle reflects two assumptions. The first assumption is that company and union exist in a hostile win-lose adversary state which somehow must be interrupted in order to initiate collaborative effort. The second assumption is that collaboration between company and union will lead naturally to the displacement of adversary relationships by some form of industrial democracy.

Neither assumption is necessarily valid. Some companies already exist in a friendly collaborative state and function with unions as mutually respectful adversaries on the usual issues of collective bargaining, such as pay, benefits, and job security. The second assumption, that collaboration is industrial democracy, is rarely correct. Most collaborative efforts between company and union represent a condition of détente, based on a compartmentalization of media into two categoreis—those which are "safe" for collaborative effort and those reserved for adversary collective bargaining. Irving Bluestone, Vice President of the United Auto Workers, lists a number of topics for joint company-union effort, including alcoholism, drug addiction, emotional problems, preretirement programs, disciplinary counseling, health and safety programs, movement of work and workers, subcontracting of work, production scheduling, introduction of technological innovations, assignment of overtime, job design, and the decision-making process. However, he points out that while this collaboration is going on, "the parties remain adversaries with regard to subjects which lend themselves more naturally to the hard business of confrontation collective bargaining," such as "wages, fringe benefits, and job security."*

Although not stated as such, Mr. Bluestone's opinions constitute an official viewpoint of most national and international union leaders on the

---

*Irving Bluestone, "A Changing View of the Union-Management Relationship," *Breakthroughs in Union-Management Cooperation*, Scarsdale, N.Y.: Work in America Institute, 1977, pp. 7-12.

subject of company-union collaboration. Implicit (usually explicit) in their statements of philosophy is the requirement that the adversary relationship be preserved at all cost. It seems a paradox to support the "every employee a manager" concept in the workplace in all respects except those relating to financial reward systems.

If it is true that company management would not allow employees to participate in a democratic process of codetermination from a common data base on equitable compensation and job-security standards, Bluestone's viewpoint is valid. In short, the international union provides the necessary political clout to wrest from the company the standards it will not provide of its own volition through a consensus process. But what may be true for some companies whose employees are represented by certain unions doesn't make it true of all companies. For instance, the reward and job-security standards in the Donnelly Mirrors Company* are established through mechanisms which put workers on the same data base as managers, from which they jointly develop the mutually interdependent productivity and pay systems. The introduction of an adversary relationship into this delicately balanced socio-economic system would serve only to hamper its productivity and dampen its cooperative spirit.

When companies do not exploit their human resources and instead are willing and able to manage democratically, Bluestone's position seems less valid. In this case, the most urgent mission of the international union is to rethink its charter. If the role of the union remains as Gompers defined it,† the uplifting of the wage earner's status, unions would be meeting their responsibility best by supporting efforts toward the self-actualization of their increasingly well-informed and well-paid constituency. The appropriate task-force model for redefining the charter of the international union would include, but not be restricted to, members from the international and local unions and representatives from business, the public sector, and the disciplines of economics and sociology.

THREE MODELS OF LABOR RELATIONS

Union-company relationships may be fitted to three models: (1) win-lose adversary; (2) collaborative adversary; and (3) industrial democracy.

Model 1 (Win-Lose Adversary)

Win-lose adversary relationships characterize the vast majority of unionized organizations. Several aspects of this model are detailed in Chapter 1. Unionism was born under this model under the leadership of Samuel Gompers (AFL), William Haywood (IWW), and other union leaders who encountered

---

*John F. Donnelly, "Participative Management at Work," *Harvard Business Review* (January-February 1977): 117-125.

†Samual Gompers, *Seventy Years of Life and Labor*, New York: Dutton, 1925.

bitter opposition to the union movement from employers, government officials, and other conservative defenders of the free-enterprise system. Early unions were attacked as socialistic and anti-American by ruthless capitalists who used the power of laws, economics, politics, and violence to crush the unions. Unions countered, of course, with similar tactics and with the help of counterbalancing legislation, after a bitter struggle spanning several decades, established a power base for perpetuating a hostile adversary relationship into circumstances which in many cases no longer justifies them. Union leaders under this model feel compelled from time to time to foment a crisis or issue which enables them to exercise their clout and thereby demonstrate their value to their constitutency.

The strike by the UAW of General Motors in 1970 was not wanted by most of the 180,000 strikers from the 96 plants affected, nor could many of them explain the reasons for it. However, the international union leadership appeared to have a need to demonstrate to the company and the workers that it had the power to bring them to their knees. Actually, the whole demonstration was a wasteful sham in which the company ultimately collaborated by lending money to the union to help tide the workers over their period of unemployment. The total episode was a vivid illustration of the extent to which top executives in the company and union shamelessly acquiesced to the tradition of win-lose gamesmanship, at the expense of the workers and the total society. The consequences of the 1970 strike were assessed tangibly by William Serrin* in terms of a variety of far-reaching impacts. General Motors lost more than $1 billion in profits and the production of 1.5 million cars and trucks. Dividends dropped from the usual $5.00 to $2.09 per share—a gap of $600 million. The union paid out $160 million in strike benefits, had to mortgage its Black Lake recreation and education center, and paid $2.5 million in interest on loans. More than 300,000 people, in addition to strikers and lay-offs, were on reduced hours. The government lost $1 billion in taxes, the nation lost hundreds of millions of dollars in retail sales, and taxpayers paid $30 million in welfare payments.

Most courses in collective bargaining for company and union alike are based on the Model 1 win-lose adversary relationships. Bargainers are taught the fine points and loopholes of the law, briefed on trends and precedents established in other bargaining situations, refreshed on the motivation principles underlying their adversary's strategies, updated on the company's financial status and the results of compensation surveys, and are encouraged to share and exchange their "tricks" for winning.

Under the philosophy engendered by Model 1, people who otherwise would harbor no malice toward one another are required by the system to become identified as either management or labor and are often required by the

---

*William Serrin, *The Company and the Union*, New York: Knopf, 1973.

adversary system to role play hostility or mistrust in their company-union relationships. Moreover, affiliational identity usually takes precedence over ethics when the two are in conflict.

Model 2 (Collaborative Adversary)

Collaborative adversary relationships are typified by the case studies of company-union relationships completed in 1953 under the auspices of the National Planning Association.* This project focused on 12 major companies chosen because of their peaceful company-union relationships. Though collaborative relationships was the primary criterion for being selected for the study, in most cases the two parties operated from separate and admittedly conflicting charters: "The employer represents, and is concerned primarily with, a property interest which, in turn, is directly related to the financial interests of a *limited* number of stockholders or owners. The interest of the employees' organization or union is primarily that of people—a greater number in most cases—and is concerned with their material, as well as their spiritual and psychological, interest and needs. . . . The two parties coexist, with each retaining its institutional sovereignty, working together in reasonable harmony in a climate of mutual respect and confidence."†

Though the companies and unions described in these case studies operated from different charters, their compatibility in sustaining industrial peace stemmed largely from their attitudes toward each other. Management accepted the collective-bargaining process, unionism as an institution, and considered a strong, democratic, and responsible union as an asset to the company. At the same time, the union respected the private ownership of industry and recognized the dependence of its members on the successful operation of business. These attitudes were conducive to prompt, mutually trustful conflict resolutions and widespread informal information sharing.

Two recent publications have provided new examples of union-company collaboration.‡ In most respects the cases described in these two booklets are contemporary examples of Model 2 collaborative adversary relationships. Irving Bluestone's position, described earlier, is typical of the viewpoint to which most of the forward-thinking union leaders subscribe. In no case are all issues of mutual concern to company and union open to democratic codetermination. Though the list of topics for collaborative effort has grown progressively, the union has clung tenaciously to wages, benefits, and job

---

*Clinton S. Golden and Virginia D. Parker, *Causes of Industrial Peace Under Collective Bargaining*, New York: Harper & Brothers, 1955.

†*Ibid.*, pp. 7, 8.

‡*Recent Initiatives in Labor-Management Cooperation*, Washington, D.C.: National Center for Productivity and Quality of Working Life, 1976; Joseph A. Loftus and Beatrice Walfish, *Breakthroughs in Union-Management Cooperation*, Scarsdale, N.Y.: Work in America Institute, 1977.

security to be negotiated through the traditional adversary process. This persevering concern for excluding a few issues from democratic resolution and administration suggests that not many union officials have become comfortable in a role of democratic facilitator. Some of them look on collaborative activities as a transitory fad and still regard the diminishing realm of confrontation as their real reason and means for being. When quality of working life becomes intermingled with bread-and-butter issues, as it did with the introduction of Scanlon plans in the Dana Corporation,* the international union was less than enthusiastic in its assessment of the program. Though the union's local constituency reacted positively to the opportunity to participate in improving productivity and the quality of work life, the international union's ostensible protest stemmed from the program's alleged excessive emphasis on productivity and plant performance. However, the workers themselves have not protested against this emphasis.

George Kuper, Executive Director of the National Center for Productivity and Quality of Working Life, summarized four conditions necessary for workable company-union cooperation:

1. The opportunity must be present for participants to address both economic and noneconomic issues in the work place.

2. The people addressing these issues must be those who are directly affected by them. Labor-management committees, for instance, permit rank-and-file workers, participating on an equal basis with management, to become involved.

3. No matter what problem is under discussion, labor and management should perceive that they both stand to gain from its solution.

4. Last, and perhaps most important, control of the program must be jointly exercised rather than kept in the hands of either labor or management alone.†

James Scearce, former Director of the Federal Mediation and Conciliation Service, summarizes the conditions for effective Model 2 collaborative adversary relationships:

Cooperation cannot be seen as a threat to the collective bargaining mechanism. It means working through the collective bargaining mechanism and within the union structure. If cooperative efforts are perceived as a threat to undermine the union's structure, or if they become a political threat to the established leadership, they won't get off the ground. Quite simply, you have to understand the real world of

---

*"The Scanlon Plan at the Dana Corporation," *Breakthroughs in Union-Management Cooperation,* Scarsdale, N.Y.: Work in America Institute, 1977, pp. 17-29.

†George H. Kuper, "New Insights in Labor-Management Cooperation," in *Breakthroughs in Union-Management Cooperation, op. cit.,* p. 6.

collective bargaining before you try to shape the ideal work place the way you think it should be.*

However, Mr. Scearce goes on to hint of the possibility of Model 3 industrial democracy evolving from patient acceptance of tradition as a non-threatening transitional process toward new patterns of managment: "American industrial society has its own values and traditions. If we operate through existing institutions, however, with patience and solid programs, people will begin to open their minds to new approaches."†

For instance, the collaborative efforts between the International Wood-workers of America and Kootenay Forest Products, as described in Appendix B, is an example of new relationships initiated through existing institutions. It illustrates an evolutionary movement from win-lose adversary to collabora-tive adversary relationships. As these Model 2 relationships establish new norms and gradually alter the perceptions and values of the participants, potential is created for evolution toward Model 3 industrial democracy.

Model 3 (Industrial Democracy)

Industrial democracy is an ideal which, to many now embroiled in win-lose adversary relationships, would seem pure fantasy and completely contrary to what they believe they know about human nature. Industrial democracy is not based on the perpetuation of a two-class system, but rather on an organizational model not unlike the free society which exists outside the factory gates. Model 3 is not a condition of détente with friendly and cooperative adversaries, but rather a matrix of conditions in the workplace in which all members of the work force have an opportunity to participate in democratic processes for the purpose of creating wealth, establishing systems for equitable sharing, for changing the climate of the organization, and for enabling them to take charge of their own careers.

Nor is industrial democracy a form of socialism or communism, but rather a set of conditions inspiring expression of the entrepreneur spirit in which responsible, creative, and productive individuals and groups reap higher rewards than the less effective members of the organization. Moreover, these conditions result in competitive advantage in the business sector and cost effectiveness in the public sector.

The culture of a workplace is strongly influenced by the interpersonal relationships within the organization, as discussed in Chapter 4. However, when people change their behavior from one style of leadership to another, the organization usually retains much of its previous flavor as a result of the inertia created by the systems installed under the preceding regime. Even when the systems are changed, changes in people's attitudes and perceptions take place slowly.

*James Scearce, "Labor-Management Cooperation: Myth or Reality?" *Breakthrough in Union-Management Cooperation*, Scarsdale, N.Y.: Work in America Institute, 1977, p. 47.
†*Ibid.*

Later in this chapter a variety of major and minor systems which affect the climate of an organization will be presented. Each of these systems carries with it a positive or negative valence. Few of these systems, functioning alone, would have a major impact on employee attitudes. However, if most of these subsystems each carry a small positive valence, the net impact in terms of employee attitudes is positive. But if most of these systems carry a small negative valence, the net effect is negative. Moreover, the interactive impact of these predominantly positive or predominantly negative factors tends to amplify their impact. A person seeking a single major cause of sour attitudes will invariably become frustrated. If the seemingly causal factor is isolated, the person may futilely introduce gimmicks to neutralize or reverse its negative valence. Thus job enrichment, when introduced by itself as a strategy for improving job attitudes, often fails because it represents only one of a vast collage of systems in the organization. For example, attempts to restructure jobs to make "every employee a manager" will not be well received by hourly employees as long as they continue to be set apart from the management class by the color of hard hats, the use of time clocks, discriminatory parking privileges, signal bells, pay check distribution schedules, and a myriad of other subtle symbols of the two-class system.

Sometimes a system is damaging to all members of the organization because of its intrinsic reductive design. This is true, for example, of the traditional authority-oriented performance-review system described in Chapter 4. However, the system may be redesigned to have developmental potential, but may still be damaging because it is not available to all members of the organization. The goal-oriented performance-review system (also discussed in Chapter 4) can, if applied only to supervisory personnel, accentuate the cleavage between management and labor to an even greater extent than the authority-oriented reductive system applied uniformly to people at all levels.

THE HUMAN FACTOR IN ORGANIZATIONAL SYSTEMS

At the close of the preceding chapter, six systems were examined—attitude surveys, company newspaper, recreational programs, job evaluation, training programs, and problem-solving task forces. These were described as media for interrupting the win-lose cycle and beginning the reprogramming of attitudes, perceptions, and habits of adversaries. This is not an exhaustive list, but rather an in-depth analysis of six specimen systems from the more comprehensive list detailed in this chapter. Though the attitude-survey system probably has the greatest potential for evoking democratic involvement in organization development, the other systems, because of their sheer numbers, collectively have greater potential as vehicles for industrial democracy.

Opportunities for joint effort are limited only by the number of systems in the organization. Be definition, a system is a process of people interacting to apply resources to achieve goals.* Systems come into existence because of the needs of people—formally or informally and officially or unofficially. When an authority figure (either company or union) unilaterally installs a formal and official system without appropriate involvement of the system users, it usually evokes the emergence of informal unofficial systems to counteract it. This psychological tug of war is a manifestation of a principle cited by Allan Mogensen that "people don't oppose change—they oppose being changed." But when people have a voluntary hand in the change process, they develop a natural proprietary interest in making it work. Thus people's attitudes and perceptions are the primary factors in making systems work. People can cause well-designed systems to fail or poorly designed systems to succeed.

When people feel they are a part of the organization, they tend to support its systems. But when they feel alienated from the organization, they tend to ignore or defeat its systems. Thus in an organization where the company and union coexist as adversaries, the union members tend to identify with the union systems and to violate company systems. Under these conditions, petty theft, absenteeism, tardiness, abuse of sick leave, waste, and slowdowns are commonplace. At the same time, people whose commitment is primarily to the organization are less supportive of systems and procedures instituted and administered by the union. Hence management tends to drag its feet on check-off procedures, grievance handling, seniority issues, and is likely to look for technical loopholes in the agreement.

Though a given system may be perceived as being primarily company or union, its impact on the workplace makes it a matter of concern to all members of the organization. Thus the administration of a company parking lot or a union newspaper may each have impact on all members of the work force.

Regardless of who sponsors it, a system will be more effective if the people who are influenced by it:

1. Understand its purpose
2. Agree with its purpose
3. Have a hand in developing it
4. Know how to use it
5. Are in control of it
6. Can influence its revision
7. Receive timely feedback from it.

THE EFFECTIVE ORGANIZATION

Under conditions of industrial democracy, the union's role is to serve as an organizational vehicle to enable its members, working together and with nonmembers, to reach consensus mutually supportive of personal and

---

*M. Scott Myers, *Every Employee a Manager,* New York: McGraw-Hill, 1970, p. 117.

organizational goals. Hence counterproductive behavior and political games-manship are minimized by the collective influence of personal commitment, peer pressure, and joint-stake concern for organizational effectiveness.

An effective organization satisfies two conditions basic to industrial democracy:

1. Its members are free to assert themselves as individuals; and

2. They are united in the pursuit of common goals.

These two conditions are inherently or potentially in conflict. Thus their satisfaction requires a delicate balance between them. This delicate balance is not attainable, of course, in an organization divided against itself by adversary company-union relationships.

As an independent entity, the union may enable its members to exper-ience these two conditions through self-expression in union activities, by establishing and protecting individual rights in the workplace, and by uniting its members in the pursuit of common goals. Unfortunately, the common goals of union members may differ from the goals of the host organization. Thus union members may enjoy these two conditions to the exclusion of the people not in the bargaining unit whose efforts may be more closely aligned with the pursuit of organizational goals. When company and union compete with each other for the allegiance of their common members, the goals of one or both are unavoidably thwarted.

The failure of industrial democracy in the unionized organization is not always wholly attributable to company-union conflict. Harmonious relation-ships may also be thwarted by conflicting motives within the organization itself and within and between unions. A plant manager, for example, who understands the interdependent relationship between employee commitment and job security may be frustrated by a corporate edict requiring layoffs. His or her subordinate role limits the opportunities to seek alternative cost-reduction strategies. Whether the cutback is initiated by plant or corporate decision has little relevance to union leaders—it is a condition they, in their traditional reactive role, must attempt to control or ameliorate.

Similarly, conflicting motives may exist between local unions and their headquarters and between or within locals in the same organization. For example, members of a local union may develop a joint-stake relationship with managers to pursue common goals, only to encounter opposition from union business representatives or international officers. For instance, a process of gradual personnel reduction through natural attrition might make sense to the members of the local union whose careers are tied to the success of the organization, but a reduction in membership may precipitate the intervention of the international union. Moreover, international officers have been known to drag their feet in the installation of motivational systems, such as Scanlon plans, stock ownership, and other sharing plans, presumably because such systems are believed to reduce local dependence on the parent union.

Jurisdictional disputes and conflicts between local union officers or officer candidates can also sidetrack productive effort. This is particularly true if company leadership fails to harness the productive potential of the work force and thus by default encourages the local union to become a medium for irresponsible and rebellious expression of talent.

Officers of corporations and international unions are seldom deliberately or maliciously self-serving, and most respond favorably to nonthreatening opportunities to develop synergistic relationships between company and union. However, cooperation should not be motivated by altruism, but rather by a pragmatic awareness that today's workers are responsive to self-actualizing work roles and are becoming less tolerant of unnecessary constraints imposed by authoritarian company or union figures.

Successful union-management collaboration is rarely achieved by restricting it to relationships among people at the top of company and union pyramids. For example, putting union leaders on the board of directors may in and of itself be but a form of tokenism which perpetuates paternalism and manipulation, which does little to facilitate the expression of creativity and initiative among the increasingly sophisticated and liberated members of the bargaining unit. Industrial democracy grows out of widespread involvement at the shop and office floor level through the development of strong, democratic, and responsible local unions.

People in high positions of company and union organizations experience an understandable uneasiness about the expression of initiative at the lower levels—however unjustified this anxiety ultimately proves to be. A union leader who opposed the installation of a Scanlon plan in a manufacturing plant acquiesced to the popular demand of his constituency, and the plan was successfully implemented. Subsequently, the plan spread to other plants in the same company. Today the same union leader has joined hands with company managers in support of the jointly installed Scanlon plans. Similarly, a division head in an electronics manufacturing plant reacted to the concept of industrial democracy with scorn and indifference. However, he became a hero when his project managers bootlegged the concepts into their engineering and manufacturing operations. His improved image resulted from his division's increased productivity and his presumed sponsorship of participative management.

In Chapter 5, the joint manager-union leader seminar was described as a medium for interrupting the win-lose cycle and for putting the adversaries on a common data base from which they could collaboratively pursue organizational effectiveness. Such an approach presumes and implies the need for a high level of sophistication in conducting such a joint workshop. However, at least one company, The Eaton Corporation, approached the problem from the perspective of company and union people planning the start-up of a new factory. Recognizing the "second-class citizenship" status of factory workers as compared to office employees, they wrote a hypothetical letter from a blue-collar worker to management, as follows.

127

Dear Sir:

What you are asking me, as I see it, is why am I not giving you my best in exchange for the reasonable wages and benefits you provide me and my family.

First, I'm not trying to blame anybody for why you don't see the "whole" me. Some of the problem is company policy, some is union thinking, some is just me. Let me tell you why, and I'll leave it to bigger minds than mine to figure out blames and remedies.

I'll begin with my first day on the job 11 years ago—my first factory job, by the way. I was 19 then. Incidentally, my cousin started work in your office as a clerk typist on the same day. We used to drive to work together. She still works for you too.

The first thing I was told that day by the personnel manager and my foreman was that I was on 90 days' probation. They were going to measure my ability and attendance and attitude and then make up their minds about me. Gee, that surprised me. I thought I'd been hired already—but I really wasn't. Although the foreman tried to make me feel at home, it was still sort of a shock to realize I was starting out kind of on the sidelines until I proved my worth. In fact, the only person who told me I "belonged," without any strings attached, was my union steward.

You know, that first day my foreman told me all about the shop rules of discipline as if I were going to start out stealing or coming to work drunk or getting into fights or horseplay. What made it even worse was then I later found out that no one told my cousin she was on probation. I asked her if she had seen the rules, and here it is 11 years later, and she still doesn't know there are about 35 rules for those of us working in the factory.

What it boils down to is that your policies—yes, and the provisions of our union contract—simply presume the factory-man untrustworthy, while my cousin in the office is held in much higher regard. It's almost like we work for different companies.

After I had been here about eight months, a car hit my car broadside on the way to work. My cousin and I were both taken to the hospital right away and released several hours later. As soon as I was released by the hospital, I called the plant to tell them what happened. I couldn't get through to my foreman, so I told my tale to a recording machine. When my cousin didn't show up by nine o'clock, her boss got worried and called the house and then the hospital. When he found out my cousin had a broken arm and some cuts, but was basically okay, he sent for a taxi to take her home.

Both my cousin and I ended up missing four days' work. On each of the next three days, I called and told the tape recorder I would not be in. I never heard from anybody in the company and when I got back to work later that week, my supervisor said, "Sure glad to see you're okay. . .it's a shame you spoiled your perfect attendance record. . . ."

Sir, I don't come to work to be worried about by someone, but I have some difficulty understanding why, when I'm absent, nobody really cares. It seems as if the company's just waiting for me to do something wrong. When I got back to work from that car accident, you started getting another little chunk less from me. Does that sound crazy? Or does it seem selfish?

Sir, why must I punch a time clock? Do you think I'd lie about my starting and quitting times? Why must I have buzzers to tell me when I take a break, relieve myself, eat lunch, start working, go home? Do you really think I can't tell time or would otherwise rob you of valuable minutes? Why doesn't the rest room I must use provide any privacy? Why do I have to drive my car over chuck holes while you enjoy reserved, paved parking? Why must I work the day before and after a holiday to get holiday pay? Are you convinced I will extend the holiday into the weekend—while, by the way, my cousin is thought to have more sense than that?

I guess I'm saying that when you design your policies for the very few who need them, how do you think the rest of us feel?

Sir, do you really think I don't care or don't know what you think of me? If you are convinced of that, then you will never understand why I bring less than all of myself to my workbench.

You know, sir, in my 11 years, I've run all kinds of machinery for you, but your company has never even let me look at what the maintenance man does when he has to repair one of my machines. No one has ever really asked me how quality might be better or how my equipment or methods might be improved. In fact, your policies drum it into me good and proper that you really want me to stay in my place. And now, *you* want to know why *I* don't pour it on? Wow! Don't you realize that I may want to contribute more than you let me? I know the union may be responsible for some of this—but again, I'm trying to explain why, not whose fault it is.

You know, sir, I would like a more challenging job, but that isn't the heart of the matter, not for me at least. If there were a sense of dignity around here, I could not hold back the effort and ideas within me, even if my particular job was less than thrilling. Many of my buddies do not want a greater job challenge, but they do want their modest contributions respected.

You know, my neighbor is a real quiet, sweet old man who just retired from here last month. When I asked him how he sums up his life's work, he said—and I can almost quote him exactly—"A pretty good place to work; only thing that really bothered me was that warning I got 26 years ago for lining up at the clock two and one-half minutes early."

Well, sir, I suspect that 26 years ago, you may have corrected this quiet, nice guy for lining up early at your clock. But the price you paid was making him a "clock watcher" for 26 years. I wonder—was that warning all that necessary? Why couldn't you have just told him why lining up early isn't a good idea and then relied on him to discipline himself? I wonder.

It has been said, sir, that factory people look upon *profit* as a dirty word. I don't feel that way, but you know, it's almost as if *love* is the dirty word here.

Why don't I give my best? Well, I guess I have a kind of thermostat inside me that responds to your warmth. Do you have a thermostat inside you?

Very truly yours*

Based on the assumed validity of this letter, policies and procedures were revised, particularly and initially in the opening of new plants. Later, as the new plants experienced significant gains in motivation and productivity, revisions were gradually introduced into the older operations. Initially the joint labor-management "Quality of Work Life Committee" consisted of four members each from management and the union. After a year of operation, the committee raised its membership to ten to include an office employee and a late-shift factory worker.

The Eaton approach is not a top-down, preplanned, standardized, and formalized program, but rather spontaneous and ad hoc measures which seem to be supportive of the principles endorsed by the committee and local plant people. Don Scobel cites the following examples as expressions of the evolving Eaton philosophy:

1. *Special invitation to regular meetings:* On an ad hoc basis, people who don't ordinarily attend are invited to sit in on such meetings as production control, supplier appraisal, engineering process, sales planning, and staff meetings. A nonsupervisory office, a factory person, a union official, and/or a foreman might be invited.

2. *Departmental meetings*: The head of a department or operation holds periodic meetings with his people to discuss things other than immediate job projects. Meetings may be participative or have guest speakers or be led by one or more of the participants.

3. *The manager's roundtable*: The manager of a facility periodically meets with someone from each major unit of the facility (usually selected on a rotating basis) to discuss matters of importance to the manager or anyone else attending. Representatives of factory and office supervision may also attend these sessions. The roundtable is often followed up with reports at departmental meetings.

4. *Supervisor's meetings*: Meetings usually involving both office and factory supervision to dispense information and to get supervisory input and feedback.

5. *Newspaper editors*: The editorship of the local facility house again is turned over to a volunteer, who may be a nonsupervisory person. Some-

---

*Donald N. Scobel, "Doing Away with the Factory Blues," *Harvard Business Review,* November-December 1975. Copyright © 1975 by the President and Fellows of Harvard College; all rights reserved.

times several volunteers form an editorial board which, within specific financial limits, has the full responsibility for the house organ.

6. *Hiring process*: Groups of applicants for nonsupervisory jobs are invited to informal meetings (often spouses are also invited) to discuss what the plant is all about and to meet and talk to supervisors, union representatives, and their future peers. They are given a tour of factory and office and later participate in a similarly conducted orientation process.

7. *Tour guides*: Tours of community groups, guests, job applicants, and present employees are conducted by volunteers from office and factory. Plant tours for families and friends may be totally planned by the employees themselves.

8. *Social-service training:* In conjunction with either local academic people and/or social-service agency people, groups of supervisors, union representatives, and other interested employees are jointly trained in spotting employee problem situations and arranging liaison with appropriate professional counsel.

9. *Educational committee*: A committee of voluntary office and factory supervisors to analyze educational resources in the community, plan, and recommend courses to meet employee needs at all levels.

10. *Departmental safety teams:* Each factory foreman and two or three members of his work group (on a rotating basis) form a departmental safety team with responsibility for safety training, accident investigation, statistical reporting, and periodic inspections. Where a plantwide safety committee exists, these local teams serve as grass roots adjuncts to the plant committee.

11. *Recreation committee*: This committee, made up of volunteers from all levels of the organization, is given specific financial resources and entrusted to design and implement the entire spectrum of recreational programs.

12. *Process-improvement team*: A team composed of engineering, factory management, and office and factory personnel encourages and reviews process-improvement ideas and plans. This committee solicits not only such ideas from the entire workplace community, but also the viewpoints of the people who would be influenced by changes proposed by professional systems designers.

13. *Improvement sharing plans*: The process-improvement team may also design an economic sharing plan to provide earnings adjustments (for everyone) based on gains in the sales/labor ratio resulting from operational improvements.

14. *Open-floor policy:* The intent here is to consider the factory person's area a legitimate place to conduct necessary office-type business when it

is effective to do so. Each office function designs its own plan to minimize the factory-office barrier.

15. *Time recording*: Mechanical time clocks are replaced by a time-accounting report to be completed by job incumbents.

16. *Evaluation of supervisors*: Factory and office supervisors optionally have their employees complete periodic supervisory-effectiveness rating forms.

17. *Food-service committee*: A committee of volunteers administers all aspects of food-service activities within a prescribed budget.

18. *Disciplinary counseling*: In place of formal disciplinary warnings and suspensions, supervisors, with the participation of the union, administer a counseling process.

19. *Work schedules*: Work groups participate in planning regular and overtime work schedules and the use of flextime.

20. *Supervisor selection:* Employees have an opportunity to influence the supervisory selection process and the selection of their own supervisor.

21. *Community-service activities*: Community-service activities, such as bond drives, Red Cross blood programs, and the United Fund, are directed and coordinated by interested volunteers from throughout the workplace society.

22. *Bells and buzzers:* Unnecessary and undesired sound signals to regiment employee behavior may be evaluated and discontinued.

None of the processes above, viewed singly, would substantially alter the culture or effectiveness of the organization. However, each of these processes or systems carries with it a small positive valence for most of the people affected by it, and collectively and interactively their impact is compounded to make Eaton a different and better place to work.

Don Scobel stresses the point that these processes are not standardized and uniformly applied in all Eaton situations. His advice to managers in a public seminar is: "You have to make your own road maps on where you want to go and how to get there; and you may have to modify your approaches as you go along to satisfy the different and changing needs of the participants." Much of the value of these processes derives from the fact that they are systems shaped by the system users, and as such they carry with them the proprietary involvement of the members of the work force. These are not "management" programs or "union" programs, but "people" programs.

Exhibit 25 illustrates the wide variety of opportunity in all organizations for inspiring commitment and productivity. However, it also shows its potential (under Model 1) for impoverishing life at work and for quashing motivation.

(N = Normal, V = Variable, S = Seldom)	Model 1: win-lose adversary	Model 2: collaborative adversary	Model 3: industrial democracy
Control of one's job			
Planning	S	V	N
Doing	N	N	N
Controlling	S	V	N
Performance review			
Evaluation	N	N	N
Feedback	S	V	N
Goal-setting	S	V	N
Reporting	S	V	N
Compensation systems			
Salaried status	S	V	N
Hourly wages	N	N	V
Automatic pay increases	N	V	S
Merit pay increases	S	V	N
Piece-work incentive	N	S	S
Paid suggestion plan	S	V	S
Contributory benefits	S	V	N
Noncontributory benefits	N	V	V
Discretionary bonuses	S	V	N
Sharing plans	S	V	N
Codetermination of pay	S	V	N
Opportunity to influence staffing functions			
Recruiting	S	V	N
Interviewing	S	V	N
Selection	S	V	N
Orientation	S	V	N
Placement	S	V	N
Training	S	V	V
Promotions	S	V	V
Discharges	S	S	V
Layoffs	S	V	N
Health and safety			
Attend meetings	V	N	N
Chair meetings	S	V	N
Establish standards	S	V	V
Monitor compliance	S	V	N
Investigate hazards	S	V	N
Recommend corrections	S	V	N
Statistical reporting	S	V	V
Host OSHA inspectors	S	V	N
Safety training	S	V	V

Exhibit 25 Employee roles under three models of industrial relations.

	Model 1: win-lose adversary	Model 2: collaborative adversary	Model 3: industrial democracy
Communication—department meetings			
Attend department meetings	V	N	N
Receive information	N	N	N
Group discussion	S	V	N
Influence meeting agenda	S	V	N
Chair meeting	S	S	V
Communication—newspaper			
Receive newspaper	N	N	N
Write to editor	V	N	N
Place ads in newspaper	V	N	N
Report news	S	V	N
Edit newspaper	S	V	N
Communication—attitude survey			
Design survey	S	V	N
Complete questionnaire	V	N	N
Receive results	S	N	N
Analyze results	S	V	N
Prepare recommendations	S	V	N
Participate in implementation	S	V	N
Receive implementation feedback	S	V	N
Communication—rank-oriented status symbols			
Parking	N	V	S
Furnishings	N	V	S
Office location	N	V	S
Dress code	N	V	S
Signal bells	N	V	S
Pay schedules	N	V	S
Eating facilities	N	V	S
Coffee service	N	V	S
Communication—democratic status symbols			
Product image	N	N	N
Landscaping	N	N	N
Architecture	N	N	N
Facilities maintenance	N	N	N
Service badges	N	N	N
Communication—miscellaneous			
Access to telephone	S	V	N
Use computer terminal	S	V	N
Open-door	S	V	N
Open-floor	S	V	N

Exhibit 25 (cont.)

	Model 1: win-lose adversary	Model 2: collaborative adversary	Model 3: industrial democracy
Access to library	S	V	N
PA announcements	N	N	N
Closed-circuit TV	V	V	V
Participate in task forces	S	V	N
Parent-Child conflict resolution	N	V	S
Adult-Adult conflict resolution	S	V	N
Read bulletin boards	N	N	N
Post bulletins	S	V	N

Exhibit 25 (cont.)

The items in Exhibit 25 are a basis for understanding the three models of industrial relations — Model 1 win-lose adversary, Model 2 collaborative adversary, and Model 3 industrial democracy. As such, it constitutes a checklist for diagnosing the current status of an organization, and a framework for developing road maps to Models 2 and 3.

The two following hypothetical situations are described to compare the life-styles of an individual in two successive jobs as he moves from one organization to another. The same international union is involved in both situations, but different bargaining units. In the first situation, Bill Smith is employed under conditions of Model 1 win-lose adversary relationships, and in the other, Bill Smith has quit his first job during a strike and has found a new job in another factory under conditions of Model 3 industrial democracy.

Bill Smith under Model 1

Bill Smith finds his assembly job in the axle plant monotonous and boring. The high points of his workday are his lunch break, coffee breaks, and leaving the plant at night. He knows his job so well he could do it with his eyes closed, and he feels that the company isn't using his talents. However, there is little opportunity to exercise his creativity and judgment on the job because industrial engineering has defined his job procedure quite explicitly and established standards which are the basis for him and his peers to earn a productivity bonus. On several occasions, he's thought of ways to improve the assembly procedure, but he knows better than to say anything, because his friends and the union steward would jump on him. If the job method changes, industrial engineering is permitted, under the terms of the union agreement, to set new standards.

He's not dissatisfied with his pay. The union negotiated a contract that guarantees him a good hourly rate, even when he doesn't make standard, and an automatic pay increase every four months. Actually Bill and most of his

135

peers make about 35 percent more than the standard rate. Under the union agreement, if the group consistently exceeds the 135 percent level of productivity, the company may change the standards. Hence Bill and his peers collaborate to make sure they do not exceed the maximum rate. Most of them do it easily and pace their activities so that the last hour of each day is devoted largely to "looking busy" on various nonproductive activities. Some of the workers overproduce, but store the overage under the bench in case of future machine breakdowns, absenteeism, and rejects by quality control.

In addition to the paycheck, Bill is entitled to 12 days sick leave per year with pay, a company-funded pension plan, a group insurance plan, and a Christmas turkey each year. He usually takes his sick leave during hunting season or during spring plowing or fall harvest time.

The only time Bill's performance is evaluated is when his productivity is too far below or too far above standard. Should his productivity remain below standard for three weeks, he may be given a warning by supervision and possibly reassigned. If he exceeds the 135 percent level, he comes under pressure from his peers and the union.

Bill was hired five years ago under guidelines established by the EEOC and was given a routine orientation by the personnel department. He was given a long list of rules governing conduct in the plant and was told that his union dues would be routinely deducted from his paycheck. Then he learned that for the first 90 days he would be on probation, during which he could be fired without recourse to the grievance procedure. His supervisor gave him a job description and told him what was expected from him on the job. He subsequently learned some conflicting union guidelines from his peers and the shop steward. But he didn't worry about it because his job was secure as long as he met minimum standards. The longer he worked with the company, the more secure he felt, as layoffs were made on a seniority basis.

However, he is painfully aware of the fact that his security is not entirely in his own hands. Two years earlier the international union struck all the plants in his division, and he was unemployed for nine weeks. The union strike fund helped for four weeks, but when it was expended, he was without income. He found a few odd jobs in the community, but he and his fellow strikers were forced into drastic changes in their spending habits. Some of them were subjected to foreclosures on autos and furniture being purchased on the installment plan. He and his friends didn't want the strike and didn't fully understand why they had to have it. The union representative pointed out that these sacrifices were necessary from time to time to keep the union strong.

About once a month he attends safety meetings conducted by the safety coordinator. Though he doesn't like the rules, which require him to wear safety equipment, he likes attending the meetings because its an opportunity to escape the job for a while. Sometimes he and his friends ask a lot of questions to make the meeting last longer.

He also attends quarterly meetings conducted by his department head. The department head shows them charts and graphs on business activities, work schedules, late deliveries, quality rejects, waste and scrap, abuse of sick leave, tardiness and absenteeism, and productivity per payroll dollar. Bill also enjoys this meeting as another escape from the job and to engage in the pleasant pasttime of whispering and snickering with his friends during the meeting. Sometimes he would like to ask questions and express his opinions, but he feels somewhat inhibited by the presence of his supervisor and shop steward. Management and office people tend to sit in the front part of the room, whereas union people tend to cluster toward the back.

Two monthly newspapers are distributed through the reading racks— one published by the company and the other by the union. The company newspaper usually consists of about ten pages and is published at the first of the month. The union newspaper comes out ten days later, usually consists of a single sheet printed on both sides, is written in a more earthy language, and often criticizes and reinterprets the contents of the previous issue of the company newspaper. Except for the classified ads in both papers, Bill pays little attention to either. Sometimes management broadcasts information over the public address system.

When he's away from the job, talking with his friends, he takes pride in pointing out the modern buildings and landscaping of his plant site. He's also pleased to be identified with their product, which is internationally recognized as one of the best. He wears his five-year service badge on the lapel of his dress jacket.

In the plant his feeling of self-esteem is diminished by the rank-oriented status symbols around him. Though his eating facilities, rest rooms, and work areas are tidy, he is surrounded by reminders of his second-class citizenship. Management and office people have their names on parking lots near their office locations, whereas he has to compete with others in the hourly paid work force for a space in the big open lot. When he's late, he has to park far from the plant, which makes him later in getting to the time clock, is unpleasant in bad weather, and handicaps him in making a fast getaway to beat the crush on the freeway. Bells, whistles, and buzzer systems signal rest breaks, lunch period, and shift changes, but office personnel seem to disregard these signals. At coffee break he meets with his peers at the coffee bar. Secretaries come out to the coffee machines to get coffee for the supervisors, and top-management people have an urn of fresh coffee wheeled into their offices.

For lunch, Bill has the option of bringing his lunch or buying one in the company cafeteria; however, toted lunches must be eaten in the cafeteria. The half-hour lunch period affords insufficient time to go off-site for lunch. Lunch groups consist of clusters of production workers, maintenance workers, office personnel, and lower-level management and supervision. People in the three upper echelons of management, with occasional customers and guests, go upstairs to the executive dining room. Though the food is prepared in the same kitchen, it is served by waiters from a menu selection. Unlike those in the cafeteria, the chairs are cushioned, dining tables have white tablecloths, and places are set with silverware, goblets, and cloth napkins. Windows are draped, lighting is subdued, and background music is playing. Though a recent directive has made the upstairs dining room available to all employees, few have chosen to use it. Workers in their khakis and blue jeans feel out of place among people in ties and jackets. Also, the prices on the menus are higher, though it is rumored that management people pay a flat monthly fee for their lunches.

Bill is paid weekly by checks distributed by his supervisor. Bill's supervisor is paid twice a month, and top-management people once a month. Supervisors' and managers' checks are in envelopes, but Bill's is not.

If Bill has a problem, he takes it up with his shop steward, who may decide to file a grievance or personally attempt to resolve it through contact with appropriate management personnel. Though it is company policy to maintain an open-door policy, it is rarely exercised, as people from the shop feel uncomfortable in the carpeted and cushioned offices of management. Also, the union insists on having a steward accompany any person who wishes to discuss a problem with management. Many problems are written up as grievances to be handled by a standard procedure, though the backlog of unprocessed grievances tends to prolong and intensify frustrations.

Two sets of bulletin boards are maintained throughout the plant—one for management and one for employees. The management bulletin board is enclosed in glass and locked. It contains legally required notices and any official bulletins management chooses to post. Others may post notices on the bulletin board if the content meets the approval of the adjacent secretary, who keeps the key, monitors and approves acceptable bulletins, and records the name and clock number of the person posting the notice and the expiration date of the notice. The employee bulletin board is a large unenclosed piece of cork board which anyone can use at will. As a consequence, it is in a chronic state of compressed disarray, with a mixture of current and obsolete notices and classified ads. The union also uses this board and will usurp the space in the upper left corner for union announcements.

All in all, Bill Smith's life isn't bad compared to that of most of the people who work with him in the plant. Nor is his life bad compared to that of workers in totalitarian and underdeveloped countries. However, compared to the people in management, supervision, and office, his life is bad. He is well enough informed to know that he is inescapably held in a dependency relationship to management and the union. The job offers little opportunity for growth, achievement, responsibilty, and recognition. The job is simply a form of punishment to be endured to get the money necessary for what is really important—away from the job.

Unfortunately, things didn't continue as he hoped. A year later the union contract expired, and as a result of breakdown in negotiations, Bill and his peers sustained a long strike. In desperation, Bill sought a job elsewhere and succeeded in getting one in another town in an axle factory where his job skills were relevant.

The same union existed in the new plant, but as he was to learn later, it was a different local with a different philosophy. Also, Bill was somewhat puzzled by the hiring procedure. He was screened with other applicants by the personnel department and introduced to the work group where the opening existed. They talked to him as a group and individually, and after a few days a member of the group called him and told him that they had chosen him—if he was still interested.

Bill Smith under Model 3

Bill Smith finds his job in the axle plant interesting and challenging. Being a member of a team involved in solving problems, setting goals, troubleshooting, rearranging priorities, dealing with emergencies, and resolving conflict puts a whole new perspective on life. It's true that he lost six years of seniority when he left his previous job, but that fact is less important and relevant in his new situation, as the union supports the concept of merit over seniority as a basis for job security.

As he thinks back to his job interview two years ago when he obtained his new job, the things that puzzled him at that time are now understandable. His peers explained to him during the interview how they worked together as a team and how important it was for every member to be there when needed and how necessary it was for them to get along well with one another. When he asked them what kind of boss they had, they told him that the "boss" doesn't act like a traditional boss or supervisor, but rather acts as, and is referred to as, the team advisor.

When they asked him if he thought he could work as a cooperative member of their team, he assured them that he would like to try. Being out of a job and hard-pressed financially, he was willing to promise anything, even though he didn't at that time understand the full significance of what they were asking.

He and his teammates are in charge of production planning and scheduling, as well as the usual fabrication and assembly work he did in the other plant. In addition, they are in charge of quality control and are the first to receive feedback from customers and other functions when quality problems arise. Their team leader meets with them regularly at the beginning of each work week and on an ad hoc basis when necessary to assist them in establishing priorities and targets for the coming week. Much of the time the team advisor runs interference for them, seeing to it that they have supplies, equipment, personnel, and information necessary to do their jobs.

Occasionally, special meetings are set up in which production employees from their own and other departments, team advisors, engineers, project managers, customer representatives, sales personnel, and suppliers all participate. These meetings may focus on a variety of cost, schedule, quality, design, performance, and coordination problems. Such meetings enable a work team to understand its responsibility within the context of the total plant mission. It also enables team members to get acquainted with other functions and the people who work there. This working together across functions and levels is a bridge for establishing natural first-name relationships. He was surprised at first to learn that local union rules permitted crossing craft lines.

Team members break the monotony at times by swapping jobs. They needn't get permission from the team advisor or union shop steward, but act under guidelines which require that job changes be voluntary by the job incumbents and that any person relinquishing his or her job to another is accountable for the replacement's competence to handle the job.

Bill is impressed by the fact that productivity is so much higher in this plant than it was where he worked before. Though the actual output of units is only about 20 percent higher than the other plant, the net cost of producing them is much lower, due to fewer rejects and less scrap. Moreover, they meet delivery schedules more consistently and rarely have to work overtime to accomplishment it.

They are not paid on a piece-work incentive basis, but receive a salary based on a 40-hour week. They keep their own time and at the end of the work week report any deviations from standard. They usually work eight hours per day, five days per week, but may depart from this pattern under a flextime schedule. They may come in as early as 7:00 A.M. and work as late as 6:00 P.M. and come in on Saturday if necessary. Most of them work from 8:00 to 4:00 P.M. each day and depart from this schedule by coordinating their deviations with peers on their own and other shifts. Except for the periods when all are expected to be on hand, such as for the Monday morning staff meeting, they may come and go during the day within the constraints imposed by the production schedules. Occasionally, an individual will swap shifts with another person if it is to their mutual advantage to do so. They coordinate their flextime schedules with their teammates and team advisor, not so much for the purpose of getting authority, but rather for the purpose of keeping the team informed and viable.

Two persons working on the same job may receive different amounts of salary. Under the merit pay system, a higher achiever receives higher merit increases than do lower achievers. Though an above-average achiever will ultimately reach the top of the rate range, he or she will stay at the top only if job performance merits it. When rate schedule adjustments are made, individuals move up in the rate only on the basis of merit. Hence a former high achiever at the top of the old range, whose performance has deteriorated, may receive no increase at the semiannual review. In contrast, a lower-paid newcomer whose achievement warrants it may receive a substantial increase which moves him or her proportionately higher in the rate range. High achievement is determined by composite peer and team advisor ratings which take into consideration productivity, creativity, and cooperativeness. The actual criterion against which they rank order one another is "which of these persons is making the greater contribution to the success of our organization?" Hence relative salary level may be in a continuous state of flux over a period of several years.

At the year-end review, outstanding performers may receive a discretionary bonus. High achievers at the top of their rate range who may be making disproportionately higher contributions to the success of the organization may receive a bonus of one or more week's salary. These awards, which are usually granted to less than five percent of the high achievers at all job grade levels, circumvent the limitations imposed by rate ranges without distorting the job-evaluation structure. Recipients of discretionary bonuses are identified by a consortium of team advisors with the involvement of the next level of management and the personnel department.

The third source of income is the Scanlon plan, which affects all persons at their plant site. Unlike merit increases and discretionary bonuses, which are keyed to individual contribution, the Scanlon plan pays off on teamwork. Savings from labor, materials, and operating supplies are a collective basis for calculating monthly bonuses awarded to every member of the plant site as a percent of current salary. Hence all members of the work force are involved, and there is nothing to be achieved by simply moving an expense from one budget to another. Bill noted that unlike his previous job, where peer pressure suppressed high productivity and the outstanding performer, peer pressure here encourages high performance and cost effectiveness.

Because of the widespread involvement in, and concern for, productivity on the part of all employees, the climate of the work force is different. The Monday and Friday absenteeism which plagued his previous employer is not in evidence here. Moreover, there is not the mad rush for the parking lot at the end of the shift. One factor, of course, is flextime, which staggers arrival and departure times. Also, there are no reserved parking places for any member of plant work force, so the opportunity for shop people to find a convenient spot is enhanced. One nearby lot is reserved for the physically handicapped, car-pool drivers, or any person whose job requires the use of his or her auto three or more times per week.

Every June and December Bill and his team members review their achievements and establish new six-month goals. They begin as a group, with their team advisor as coordinator, reviewing and critiquing the past six months' accomplishments and then establishing group goals and priorities for the next six months. When they have reached consensus and each person has recorded the group work on his or her individual copy of the performance review form, the team advisor schedules a private interview with each member of the team. Individuals are encouraged to add to the group work any achievements, goals, and problems unique to them as individuals. After the individual interviews are completed, the total team is reconvened, and monthly thereafter, to coordinate their efforts and update their goals and strategies.

Bill likes the freedom people have to talk to anyone, without objections from a supervisor or union steward. At rest breaks, people from all levels mingle at the coffee bar, including the plant manager and union business representative, and there are no rules against striking up a conversation with the higher-ups. Bill finds this easy to do because the managers dress informally, as he does, and one's rank is not denoted by a dress code. They also share the same cafeteria and sometimes find themselves seated beside office, management, and maintenance personnel. Their department meetings are conducted in the same informal manner, with open discussion on a variety of topics, some of which were put on the agenda by individuals from the work teams.

The annual attitude survey, or "work-improvement survey," as they call it, is another opportunity for people to register opinions by completing the anonymous questionnaire and by participating in task forces to analyze results and prescribe remedial actions. Once a year Bill's team and the team advisor have an opportunity to review the questions on the survey form and suggest revisions. Many of the recommendations coming out of the improvement survey result in specific actions which they as a team can implement.

The plant newspaper is run entirely by plant employees. The editor, associate editor, typist, and printer are all nonsupervisory employees, as are 18 of the 27 reporters. All are volunteers; they receive no extra compensation or time away from the job for their contributions to the paper. The editor is elected by the 27 reporters. Bill was very favorably impressed by the quality of the newspaper and by the fact that the elected editor was a production worker. One of his editorials, presented in Exhibit 26, made a vivid impression on Bill because it represented a sharp contrast to the viewpoint of his fellow workers at his previous place of employment.

Knowing the editor personally made the message more readable and interesting. But coming from anyone in this plant, it would have been acceptable, but as a sermonizing message from management in his old plant, it would have been highly objectionable.

Bill is proud of his plant site and products, as he was before, but when he brags to friends and relatives about his company, it's mostly about it as a good place to work, where one is treated with dignity and respect by people at all levels. His job is not an ordeal to be endured in exchange for his salary, but rather a part of his life that he looks forward to each day with the same enthusiasm that he pursues hobbies, home life, recreation, and community activities.

WHO IS THE BOSS?

Here is a question you could ask a thousand working people and never get the right answer. Who is your boss?

There's only one boss, and whether a person shines shoes for a living or heads the largest corporation in the world, the boss always remains the same. The boss is the customer. Here is the one person who pays everyone's salary and decides whether a business is going to succeed or fail. And he does not care how long a business has been around, the minute it starts treating him badly, he will put it out of business.

This boss, the customer, has bought and will buy everything you have or will ever own. He's bought all of your clothes, your home, your car, pays for children's education, your vacations, your bills, and he pays them in the exact proportion to the way you treat him.

The man who works deep inside a big plant on an assembly line might think he's working for the company that writes his pay check. He's not—he's working for the person who buys the product at the end of the line. And if the person doesn't like the product, it won't be bought. Eventually, if this continues, he fires the man on the assembly line. In fact, he'll fire everyone in the company from the president on down. He can do it by simply spending his money some place else.

That is the reason why taking pride in the work we do is so important to us personally. Aside from the job that comes from doing a good job, it will help us get more customers, keep the one's we have and insure the pay check.

Some of the largest companies that had flourishing businesses a few years ago are no longer in existence. They couldn't or didn't satisfy the customer. THEY FORGOT WHO'S THE BOSS. . . .*

Exhibit 26 Editorial from employee newspaper: "The Editor Speaks," by Mitchell Young.

Three years after Bill Smith changed jobs, his team advisor was promoted to business manager—the equivalent of superintendent status in his old company. Their team advisor's opening was posted, as all openings are, on the bulletin board. Bill and six other people from the plant bid on the job. The seven candidates were interviewed by the members of Bill's team, and Bill was chosen to be their team advisor.

---

*Mitchell Young, "Who is the boss?" *Linde Torch*, Vol. 10, No. 3, Florence, S.C.: Linde Division, Union Carbide Corporation, March 1977, p. 3. Reprinted by permission.

CONCLUSION

On the surface, industrial democracy may appear to eliminate the need for collective bargaining and adversary encounters. Such is not the case, though it does change the form of collective bargaining and the circumstances which make adversary roles appropriate.

Life itself consists largely of transactions or negotiations between two or more people. In a broad sense, transactions are a form of bargaining—whether one is exchanging money for services or goods, affirmation for friendship or love, cooperation for solidarity, reciprocity for mutual respect, responsibility for freedom, achievement for recognition, tolerance for tranquility, or altruism for self-esteem.

As noted in Chapter 4, transactions may be authoritarian (Parent-Child) or democratic (Adult-Adult). Parent-Child transactions, which characteristically are manifested as negative strokes, evoke the win-lose posture of "I'm OK, you're not OK." Adult-Adult transactions, in combination with positive strokes, support the win-win relationship of "I'm OK, you're OK."

Traditional collective bargaining is based on a dependency relationship between the members of a bargaining unit and their union leaders and company managers. This Parent-Child relationship, of course, spawns win-lose negotiating processes between company and union. Management and labor each tend to respond from the position "We're OK, you're not OK."

Conditions of industrial democracy are undermined by Parent-Child negotiations. By definition, industrial democracy is negotiation at its best and is comprised of a balanced mixture of predominantly Adult-Adult and Child-Child transactions. When all members of the organization operate from a common data base of constraints, goals, and opportunities, unrealistic demands are less likely to be made to provoke defensive and unrealistic counteroffers.

This is not to say that differences or disagreements do not exist under conditions of industrial democracy. Conflicting viewpoints exist in every type of organization. However, industrial democracy allows disagreement to surface naturally and spontaneously as a means of reaching consensus. These conditions include a climate of mutual respect, mutual concern, good listening, open discussion, candid feedback, commitment to common goals, and a sense of humor.

Managers who do not provide these conditions wonder why engineers, civil servants, school teachers, and other "professionals," who were previously identified with management, are increasingly engaged in adversary bargaining. The answer, of course, is that mangement has reacted to their enlightened brashness by treating them more like members of traditional bargaining units in terms of circumscribed job responsibility, without providing legitimate appeal mechanisms through which Adult negotiations can take place. Hence the common complaint is heard that people in the union have the clout to get recognition and benefits, whereas people not in the bargaining unit are taken for granted and lose relative status in the organization. People in any function, at any level, who are treated like children will, of course, behave like children. Conversely, people who are treated like adults tend to respond as adults.

Translated into practice, industrial democracy finds expression through overlapping horizontal, vertical, and diagonal slices of people throughout the organization, coordinating a matrix of mainstream and staff-support efforts. Just as task forces unite people from research and engineering, production, maintenance, sales, and administration to improve customer satisfaction, similar task forces operating from the data base of wage and salary administration (community and industry surveys, job evaluation, budgetary allocations, business forecasts, shareholder or taxpayer expectations, and merit criteria) are capable of evolving pay and benefit packages compatible with the needs of the organization and its members.

The adversary relationship as a normal ongoing posture is not conducive to democratic conflict resolution in any realm of conflict. To rule that democratic relationships may govern the resolution of problems related to health and safety, job design, and assignment of overtime, but not issues related to benefits and job security is tantamount to a husband-wife agreement to love each other only on even-numbered days. This is not to say that conflict should never arise between husband and wife. Conflict is inevitable and necessary to the democratic process. But conflict handled through a democratic process does not nullify the relationship of mutual trust and respect which is the foundation for a compatible relationship.

In courts of law, an adversary relationship comes into existence between the prosecutor and defendant as a consequence of an alleged injustice. However, this relationship exists only until the focal conflict is resolved through a mutually acceptable due process of law. Though hostilities sometimes persevere following the judgment, perpetual animosity is not the intended or normal consequence of the conflict-resolution process.

Moreover, conflict in society is not restricted to relationships between upper and lower classes. More often conflicts arise among peers of any class. The traditional industrial model for conflict resolution, based on the polarization of management and labor, is not only unprepared to deal with conflict outside the bargaining unit involving, say, scientists, vice-presidents, or secretaries, but is not even prepared to resolve conflict among peers in the bargaining unit. Such conflict is usually presumed to be management's problem to be resolved under the watchful adversary eye of the union. Hence in the absence of industrial democracy, people not in the bargaining unit are subject to the whim of arbitrary authority. And justice for the members of the bargaining unit is largely a function of the clout which their union carries and the personal philosophy of their union leaders.

Enlightened union leaders often find themselves playing a role which violates their personal convictions. They see the adversary role as an impediment to the synergistic application of talent in the organization. Moreover the traditional company-union posture fosters immaturity among members of the bargaining unit, expressed as conformity to union folklore, which includes opposition to managerial innovation. But enlightened union leaders, pursuing a career in union leadership, are understandably reluctant to jeopardize their image by supporting what their constituencies perceive as a promanagement viewpoint.

However, as noted earlier, people do not oppose change—they oppose being changed. The union leader who involves his or her constituency in the change process could develop a more constructive outlet for their talent while gaining personal support as their leader. A candidate for union office campaigning on the basis of misunderstood concepts of industrial democracy is likely to be defeated. But the same person running for office on a platform of industrial democracy, which the membership helped develop, would have a competitive advantage.

Though local unions may develop synergistic relationships with their host organizations, such relationships tend to be fragile unless they are supported by officials in union headquarters. Conflict between union headquarters and local unions usually leads to either abortion of the collaborative effort or decertification of the local union.

The survival of the international union as a constructive force in society requires the introspective involvement of its officials in developing a viable charter for self-renewal. Such a charter must, of course, be simultaneously supportive of productivity and conducive to the self-actualization of its members. The values of some union leaders represent obstacles to such a constructive pursuit. However, the involvement of rigid zealots in the creative process may be the most potent and the only realistic process for unfreezing their values and for evoking their commitment to new strategies.

Appendix A

Labor Relations
in West Germany
and Sweden*

West Germany, with a population of about 62 million, occupies a land area almost the size of Oregon. Sweden's population of eight million covers an area almost double the size of Oregon. In terms of population density Sweden has about 46 people per square mile, twice the density of Oregon and about the same as that of Mississippi. West Germany has 30 times the population density of Oregon, with 645 people per square mile, comparable to that of Massachusetts.

Both countries are highly dependent on imports and must be competitive internationally. Swedish labor costs have been escalating annually at the rate of about 20 percent compared to approximately 6 percent for West Germany. Both Sweden and West Germany are oriented toward free enterprise. Despite Sweden's socialistic image, only three percent of industry is owned by the state. In both countries employer and employee organizations are centralized for collective-bargaining purposes.

COMPANY-UNION SUPERSTRUCTURE

Sweden

In Sweden the dominant employer organization in the private sector is the Swedish Employes Confederation (SAF). It is comprised of 43 affiliated employer associations representing virtually all private industry. SAF requires every member company to submit a draft of any collective agreement

---

*Information in this appendix has been abstracted from three primary sources: (1) J.F. Allison, H.D. Carruthers, B. K. Koken, J. B. O'Reilly, G. J. Towill, and S. R. Wiltshire, *Views of the Pulp and Paper Industry Concerning Labor Management Relations in Canada*, Montreal: Canadian Pulp and Paper Association, 1977, 87 pages; (2) N. Foy and H. Gadon, "Worker Participation: Contrasts in Three Countries," *Harvard Business Review*, May-June 1976, p. 71; (3) G. S. McIsaac, "What's Coming in Labor Relations?" *Harvard Business Review*, Sept.-Oct. 1977, p. 22.

147

for ratification by SAF's board before it can be signed. The SAF is a tightly knit organization providing a multitude of services to its members and exercising authority over them on a variety of matters such as the administration of collective agreements, certain working conditions and social issues, and the prevention or ordering of lockouts. In the public sector the government is represented by the National Collective Bargaining Office (SAV), which performs functions similar to those of the SAF.

The central trade union organization in Sweden is comprised of three autonomous groups which operate under similar guidelines and collectively represent about 70 percent of the total work force. The Confederation of Trade Unions (LO) represents 1.6 million manual workers, the Central Organization of Salaried Employees (TCO) about 750,000 white-collar workers, and the Federation of Professional Employees (SACO) about 120,000 members. SACO is primarily a civil service organization, but LO and TCO are strongly represented in both the private and public sectors.

West Germany

In West Germany the Confederation of German Employers Associations (BDA) represents employers who employ about 80 percent of the workers in the private sector. Though it does not impose the same degree of control over the collective-bargaining process as its counterpart in Sweden does, it does coordinate the bargaining activities of its members through a Committee on Co-Determination of Wage and Collective Bargaining Policy.

The German trade unions are organizationally more unified than the Swedish in that the German Trade Union Federation (DGB), with about 7.5 million members, represents about 85 percent of all unionized employees. The DGB acts as the voice, service center, and coordinator of wage policies for the 16 industrial unions which comprise it. Other central labor organizations are the German Federation of Salaried Employees (DAG), with 450,000 members, and the Civil Service Union (DBB), with about 700,000 members. German unions are concentrated primarily in the key industrial sectors and in public administration and represent about 35 percent of potential membership. However, the collective agreements negotiated by the 16 DGB unions directly or indirectly affect 85 percent of all West German wage and salary earners.

MECHANISMS FOR CONSENSUS

Sweden

In Sweden employer and employee central organizations work from commonly agreed on economic models including wage statistics, forecasts of trends in productivity and prices, as well as surveys of membership opinion on various issues. They each draw their own conclusions concerning wage raises that will be consistent with national economic aims of full employment, economic growth, reasonable price stability, a more even income distribution, and a positive balance of trade.

Experts on both sides, who have received similar professional training and apply the same research methods, thus seem to contribute toward a more rational approach to wage determination by enabling the parties to start centralized bargaining with a common body of facts and a better appreciation of the wider social and economic impact related to their activities.

The centralized negotiations between SAF and LO result in joint recommendations to affiliates on both sides to make national agreements within the centrally laid-down framework. Thus the central negotiations have the effect of coordinating the various negotiations throughout the country at industry level. In so doing they promote a uniform wage development and standardize other terms of employment. Thus the basic economic framework agreements are negotiated between SAF and LO, but the national unions within the LO and the employer associations within SAF are formally and legally the contracting parties.

The parties agree on the use of the economic model to reach an economic consensus, and one of its tenets is that the sector more vulnerable to international competition should be the "wage leader." With rare exceptions, bargaining in the public sector in Sweden follows patterns set in the private sector, and this is accepted by both parties as the proper relationship.

Until recently, it was the policy of both the employer and trade union organizations to avoid legislative interference in the labor market, giving preference to voluntary agreements. However, under trade union pressure new legislation was passed, including the Co-Determination Act of 1976. This act provides only a framework, leaving details to be negotiated between the bargaining partners. The act includes the following provisions:

1. Before any strategic planning or administrative action is taken with respect to any important managerial change, the employer must consult with the trade union with whom a collective agreement has been signed. With regard to certain changes, the union has ultimate veto power if it deems the proposed changes to be in conflict with the law or the collective agreement.

2. In the case of disputes concerning interpretation of agreements, the trade union's interpretation takes precedence until the disputes are settled.

3. The act puts the obligation on the employer to take the initiative for negotiations with the local union.

West Germany

In Germany collective-bargaining procedures are similarly centralized. DGB and BDA coordinate the collective-bargaining activities of their respective affiliates.

149

Unlike the Swedish system, neither of the West German organizations engages directly in negotiations as do the SAF and LO. However, the national unions and the employers associations in various industries who conduct the actual negotiations on an industry-regional basis rely heavily on the advice, guidance, expert assistance, and coordinating influence of their central associations.

Both parties are influenced by economic-consensus mechanisms which are backed by elaborately staffed economic and social research. For instance, a Council of Economic Advisors, an autonomous body of five respected economists appointed by the Chancellor, produces an annual report on the performance of the economy, with short-term forecasts for the next year in relation to national goals, full employment, balance of payments, and other relevant matters. The government responds to the council's report with its own annual statement on the economic state of the nation. These two reports constitute the basis for discussion between the parties. As a result, they arrive at the bargaining table with a good appreciation of the economic and social realities of the times and a clearer understanding of the constraints which national objectives impose.

The industry-regional bargaining process results in agreements on broad issues of wages and salaries, working conditions, and benefits. These agreements develop through pattern following, from industry to industry and region to region once an initial pattern-setting agreement has been reached.

CO-DETERMINATION

Works Councils

The broad guidelines established through the industry-regional bargaining process comprise a framework from which collective agreements are negotiated by the unions. However, West German unions at the plant level have a relatively small role, as the works councils are the primary mechanisms for implementing collective agreements. Employers deal with the unions on a centralized basis in collective bargaining, but on the plant level they deal with the work force through the works councils.

The works council is not a joint body, but represents nonmanagerial employees exclusively. Candidates for membership do not have to be union members. They are elected for three years in a secret ballot by all employees of the organization. At the local level union representatives are relatively less influential than representatives of the works council. Works councils ensure that all employees are treated equally and fairly and that acts of Parliament, regulations, safety rules, collective agreements, and work agreements are observed; they also promote the employment of the elderly and disabled.

Works councils in both Sweden and Germany have a responsibility to see that the terms of the collective agreements are implemented at the shop level.

In addition, works councils can negotiate shop agreements covering matters not included in the collective agreements, but they do not have the leverage of the right to strike. Many of the matters dealt with by works councils in West Germany and Sweden are covered by labor agreements or by union-management committees in the United States and Canada.

Members of works councils enjoy special protection and certain privileges to make them independent and efficient in their function. They cannot be dismissed by the employer while holding office. In larger companies, the chairman and other members of the works council are exempted from production work in order to devote all of their time to council matters. The employer must provide appropriate facilities for the works council and must defray all costs arising out of the council's activities.

In companies employing more than 100 workers, the works council appoints an economic committee of between four and eight members. This committee has access to information on all important matters, including manufacturing methods, automation, production programs, and the financial situation of the company.

If there is a deadlock between employer and works council on matters where the works council is entitled to co-determination, either side can bring the case before a joint arbitration committee, under an independent chairman, for compulsory arbitration.

The works council system has been an effective medium for communication and rapport in both countries for many years. Both union and management freely admit that it has fostered good attitudes through participation by employees in decisions affecting their work environment.

Board Representation

In addition to worker participation in works councils, West German workers also participate on the supervisory board. Unlike the single-board Anglo-American system, German companies have two boards—a supervisory board and an executive or management board. The supervisory board appoints the management board, scrutinizes company accounts, and is responsible for all major policy decisions; the management board conducts the day-to-day business of the company.

Under the Co-Determination Act, German workers have board representation as follows. In all organizations with more than 2000 members and in smaller companies in the coal and steel industry, parity with shareholders, with a neutral chairman; in all other companies of between 500 and 2000 employees, one-third representation. Of the employee representatives, up to three may be union officials from outside the enterprise, and at least one must represent the middle-management group. In Sweden the right to board membership exists in companies with 100 or more employees, and only employees of the firm may be directors. In both countries company and union jointly provide training for employee-directors before they take office.

The chairman is elected by a vote of all members of the board. If the necessary two-thirds majority is not attained, the chairman is elected by the shareholder representatives, and the vice-chairman is elected by the representatives of the employees. In the event of a deadlock among board members, the chairman has a second and deciding vote, thereby maintaining the balance of decision-making power in the hands of the shareholder representatives.

THE ROLE OF GOVERNMENT

Sweden

Throughout their history, the basic relationship between labor and management in Sweden has been governed by voluntary agreements rather than by law. The parties have indicated that they do not wish government intervention, and it appears that the strength of the contracting parties, together with their widespread coverage, gave them the stability to render them effective in decision making and control. Only since about 1970 has government shown a tendency to increase legislative intervention. This has been done under pressure from the unions, and notwithstanding this intervention, the character of the legislation is largely directive, leaving to the parties the responsibility for implementation. Even in such fields as employee health and safety, legislation has tended to confirm practices already developed under joint agreement.

Legislation in the labor-relations field is federal, but the administration of all legislation is done by administrative boards, which are independent of the ministries. A significant feature in the legislative process in Sweden is the extent and depth of consultation, with trade unions, employers associations, and all interested parties.

West Germany

It has been a basic principle of German labor legislation that the bargaining partners should regulate themselves. The passage of labor legislation and labor law was originally the role of the provinces, which still have authority in this field. However, when the federal jurisdiction legislates in the same field, it takes precedence, and today most labor legislation emanates from the federal government. Historically, the government has limited itself to legislating minimum standards based on the practice in larger industries. Implementation and administration of a federal labor law are the responsibility of the provinces.

The labor-law system in Germany is governed by a few clearcut principles: the individual's right to freedom of association, social protection of the individual worker, self-regulation by the two sides involved, and participation of workers in the decision-making process at plant and management levels. Underlying these general principles is the legislation dealing with collective agreements, which recognizes unions for the purpose of negotiations and which makes collective agreements enforceable at law. The enforcement of collective agreements is left to the parties themselves, who may bring actions before labor courts at the district, provincial, or federal level. The labor court has power to award damages for breaches of collective agreements in the full amount of the loss suffered.

PHILOSOPHY OF LABOR-MANAGEMENT RELATIONSHIPS

The principle of the right of employees to organize and to bargain collectively has been accepted by all parties in Sweden and West Germany for many years. As the right to organize is not a matter of contest, these countries do not have certification procedures as they are known in the United States and Canada and are not involved in the highly volatile questions of union security. Nor do they require the "right to work" laws and the statutory restrictions against closed shops current in the United States. It is interesting to note that in Germany and Sweden, where employees enjoy the complete right to associate or not, the level of union membership is higher than it is in the United States and Canada, where closed shops can exist.

In both Sweden and West Germany, the institutions and processes of collective bargaining are highly centralized. The effect of this centralization has been to produce on both the union and employer sides strong and independent organizations characterized by professionalism, internal discipline, and financial strength. Thus constituted, with a basic and functional security, these organizations are able to direct their efforts to realistic, long-term objectives. The centralization of bargaining results in less fragmentation of unions at both the plant and industry levels. In the North American system multiunion representation contributes to excessive industrial conflict.

CONTRAST HIGHLIGHTS

Bargaining processes in Sweden and Germany contrast with those in the United States and Canada as follows:

1. Sophisticated research and economic analysis mechanisms in the central organizations;

2. Widespread acceptance by unions, works councils, and employees of the need for industry to be competitive and generate profits;

3. The ability of the unions, employers, and the government to reach a consensus on what the economy will reasonably bear;

4. The flow-through impact of the framework agreements reached by the top-level organizations includes the ban on strikes at the local level.

153

5. A collective agreement becomes the "law" of the contracting parties and imposes a peace obligation on them which, by and large, is respected.

6. Central bargaining is not hindered by the necessity to resolve what are essentially local issues. These are handled at lower levels, thus leaving central negotiators free to deal with the framework issues.

7. Although the union negotiates the collective agreement, it is generally administered by the works council, which in practice is oriented to the needs of all employees and the interest of the enterprise.

COMMENT

Labor relations in West Germany and Sweden are clearly examples of Model 2 collaborative adversary labor relations. In both cases they are based on a management-labor dichotomy and the unquestioned acceptance of the adversary relationship between the two parties. In both countries the parties operate from a jointly developed and accepted information base and are committed to the concept of codetermination.

The West German model inches a bit closer to Model 3 industrial democracy by having employee board members comprised of a diagonal slice from the organization rather than the horizontal slice restrictions in Sweden. West Germany also has greater potential for approaching Model 3 by virtue of the mixed composition of its works councils, which do not require union membership. Should this concept be extended to choose works council membership from all levels and functions of the organization, a foundation would exist for reaching Model 3 industrial democracy. Such a works council would then be, in effect, a "panel of citizens" from the workplace society, with the responsibility for monitoring the application of social and economic justice, whether the target of concern be a laborer, secretary, engineer, or manager. Because such a council would represent a diagonal or vertical slice from the organization, it would not be polarized into a management-labor dichotomy. It would be similar to a "concerned citizens' group," which sometimes forms in a free society to express views on matters of civic concern such as automobile safety, nuclear power plants, defoliation of forests, food additives, and tax legislation.

Although West Germany and Sweden are often referred to as examples of industrial democracy, a valid case can be made for a viewpoint that they are further from industrial democracy than the open and often uncoordinated brand of labor relations found in the United States and Canada. The combination of employer and union federations in West Germany and Sweden constitutes a rigid superstructure which minimizes the degrees of freedom which can be exercised by individuals in the two-party system. Moreover, the two-party superstructure reinforces and crystallizes the management-labor dichotomy as an insurmountable barrier to genuine democracy.

Though the management-labor two-class system also exists in North America, particularly in the win-lose adversary situations, it is not institutionalized throughout the culture, as it is in Sweden and West Germany. In the United States there is some nationwide coordination by the National Labor Relations Board. However, the NLRB does not create economic constraints; it merely monitors the interpretation and application of labor laws, and the states may individually exercise certain options. Canada has no central agency and in effect operates under 11 uncoordinated provincial jurisdictions.

It can be argued that the West German system is better for maintaining a viable society, as it keeps the parties within the constraints essential to international competition. If this is true in the short run, will it be true in the long run? Does the superstructure of constraints extending down to the workplace represent a form of regimentation which might ultimately quash initiative and the spontaneous expression of the entrepreneur spirit? If so, is mandatory consensus a sound foundation for sustaining a competitive advantage?

The United States and Canada must, of course, learn to operate within constraints as German union leaders and managers do, but it doesn't necessarily follow that this is best accomplished by emulating the German model. Perhaps for North Americans, with their democratic heritage, the shared data base within each organization, the joint financial stake, and the widespread opportunity for all individuals to be creative and responsible is in the long run the only workable approach for preserving the free-enterprise system.

For example, the Model 2 collaborative adversary relationships in Kootenay Forest Products, as described in the following pages, seem more appropriate for preserving the entrepreneurial societies of the United States and Canada. Evolving from a spontaneous and serendipitous concern by local employees, provincial government, union officials, community leadership, and company management, the two parties have learned to operate from a common data base to accept their respective needs and to pursue their common goals.

The Worker Participation Experience at Kootenay Forest Products*

There is an increasing interest within the International Woodworkers of America in challenging traditional work and management structures. The International Woodworkers of America (IWA), currently renegotiating a contract with the British Columbia forest industry, is demanding as part of its package a joint industry-union committee to study the feasibility of implementing industrial democracy in the B. C. forest industry.

The impetus fueling the IWA's interest in industrial democracy originated to a significant degree from its Local 1-405, which has had two of its members representing workers on the Board of Directors of Kootenay Forest Products since October 1974. The history and origin of the Kootenay Forest Products experiment thus bears some examination.

Kootenay Forest Products is a medium-sized sawmilling and plywood manufacturing complex with related logging operations employing close to 600 employees. It is located in the small town of Nelson, a single-industry town geographically isolated on Kootenay Lake in the Selkirk Mountains of southeastern British Columbia.

During the late 1960s and early 1970s, Kootenay Forest Products (then a branch of Eddy Match, a British corporation) began deteriorating at an alarming rate. The company was wracked by numerous wildcat strikes, turnover among managers was high, communication among levels of management deteriorated, proper planning ceased, capital was misappropriated, workers were laid off frequently, and the company went into the red.

Common lunchroom wisdom had it that Eddy Match was running Kootenay Forest Products into the ground and retaining it only as a tax write-off. By the end of 1973 the work force became alarmed by apparent negotiations between Eddy Match and Crestbrook Forest Industries, a

---

*By Klaus Offermann, fork lift driver, job steward (International Woodworkers of America), and member of the Board of Kootenay Forest Products. A paper delivered in Edmonton on April 29, 1977, at the Conference on Industrial Democracy, sponsored by the Department of Labor, Province of Alberta, Canada.

Japanese company. The fear and rumor prevailed that Crestbrook desired Kootenay Forest Products' timber holdings in order to meet its own timber requirements and thus would have no interest in upgrading or even maintaining the operations at Nelson.

The workers felt that between these two absentee multinationals, the social responsibility toward the community would be ignored and eventually hundreds of workers would be dumped on the scrap pile of unemployment.

The workers petitioned the New Democratic Party government of the day in the following fashion:

> We the workers of Kootenay Forest Products observe with growing concern the operation and administration of Kootenay Forest Products.
>
> In the past few years we have been subjected to repeated layoffs due to mismanagement in our logging division and the resultant shortage of suitable logs.
>
> For a number of years Kootenay Forest Products has been running at a deficit in direct proportion to the lack of investment in the maintenance and installation of required equipment.
>
> In addition to the constant pressure on workers and supervisors alike to attempt to make an unbalanced operation function smoothly and profitably, a high turnover and belligerence at management level has left Kootenay Forest Products with a history of poor industrial relations, as reflected by a phenomenal employee turnover and numerous industrial altercations.
>
> We feel strongly that Kootenay Forest Products needs a major commitment now both in terms of investment and long-range planning before the present positive lumber market levels off.
>
> Eddy Match as of yet has given no indication of such a commitment.
>
> In the interest of our future job security and Nelson's job base, we the workers of Kootenay Forest Products therefore petition you, our government, to purchase Kootenay Forest Products.

Workers from Kootenay Forest Products lobbied B. C. politicians at every opportunity, and on February 28, 1974, B. C. Cellulose, the government's forestry-holding company, purchased 100 percent of the shares of Kootenay Forest Products.

Although the immediate survival of Kootenay Forest Products as an entity was now secured, workers felt they still had to achieve two tasks. First and most important, workers wanted to help correct some of the mismanagement witnessed during prior years and thus establish once and for all the economic viability of a sawmilling and plywood complex at Nelson. Workers were tired of depressed morale due to the perpetually tenuous nature of their employment and thus desired some real input.

Second, workers, particularly in the plywood plant, desired an improvement in industrial relations. Wildcat strikes and continuous open confronta-

157

tion in the past, the only effective means of dealing with an inflexible management, seemed at odds with the urgent goal of securing the economic viability of Kootenay Forest Products. It was during this time that the plant committee of union job stewards, the workers who had been most immersed in the nexus of industrial strife, started asking basic questions about the autocratic work structure they were stuck in. The question began to be asked if there could not be a work structure conducive to realizing a worker's potential more fully.

As a result of the government's desire to refrain from interfering in the day-to-day management of Kootenay Forest Products, workers soon realized that public ownership didn't necessarily change their day-to-day work situation. The management with whom they dealt was essentially unchanged. It was therefore decided by the workers that it was desirable to have input at the top levels of management.

On March 16 a "job bash" was held by the Kootenay Forest Products workers to celebrate the public ownership of the company. Bob Williams, then Minister of Lands and Forests, was invited and came. Williams had been quoted in a February 1974 *Rampart's* article as saying: "We will have worker and community representatives on the boards of Crown corporations and will also give workers some equity participation. ... This could mean that we could find an alternative way in terms of sharing wealth between management and labor instead of the kind of sterile confrontations and shut-downs and games-playing. That will take time, trust, and experience, but if it doesn't happen, much of the real purpose for public involvement in companies would disappear; just owning it to make money isn't quite good enough even for the public."

In response to his welcoming speech, one of Kootenay Forest Products' workers quoted Williams from the *Rampart's* article and challenged the government to initiate an experiment in worker participation at Kootenay Forest Products. Within a few months the government, through B. C. Cellulose, asked Local 1-405 of the International Woodworkers of America for a list of names of persons whom they might consider as representatives on the Board of Directors of Kootenay Forest Products.

The local union in its wisdom decided first and foremost that these persons should be selected from the crews of Kootenay Forest Products and should not be full-time union business agents. It was also decided that the mechanics of selecting the nominees be left up to the Kootenay Forest Products sublocals.

The plywood and sawmill union committees decided that nominees would be selected by in-plant elections. Eight nominees, representatives of bush, plywood, and sawmill crews, were selected and submitted to B. C. Cellulose. Two directors, Gary McCandlish, millwright, and Klaus Offermann, fork lift driver, were appointed from the pool by the government.

The Board of Directors of Kootenay Forest Products now consisted of three company officials, including the president, two B. C. Cellulose representatives, including the chairman of that government holding company, and two workers—a total of seven directors.

McCandlish and Offermann's appointment took place during perhaps the most difficult period of Kootenay Forest Products' tumultuous history. The North America lumber market entered one of the worst market slumps in history. Employee and lower-management morale were at rock bottom. Layoffs were on the horizon. Decisions had to be made 20 miles from Nelson on a major capital expenditure which could jeopardize the job security of workers at the Nelson sawmill. Workers opposed the project and were skeptical about the good intentions of a management placed into the context of New Democratic Party public ownership. Many workers considered the lay-offs, the obvious mismanagement, and the inflexible attitude toward workers as acts of management sabotage.

Upon our appointment to the Board of Directors, Gary McCandlish and I decided upon a number of guidelines that we would attempt to adhere to in order to facilitate both our credibility and effectiveness. First, we deemed it necessary to oppose any possible remuneration for our function. If we had been remunerated in spite of our opposition, the fees would have been placed into a fund controlled by workers, for the purpose of researching questions relating to worker alienation and industrial democracy.

We felt it to be essential that no Kootenay Forest Products worker have a reason to question our motives for acting as directors. We considered a worker-director bettering himself financially as having obvious potential for co-opting him. We were extremely conscious of the perennial bogey man of worker-director co-option raised in the past, by trade unions in particular.

Our policy would also ensure that no future candidate for worker-director vacancies would seek those positions for the purpose of receiving extra income.

Next, we decided to refrain from by-passing any established union management structures. In the case of grievances, for example, we would not involve ourselves in our capacity as directors until all steps of grievance procedure were exhausted or unless the union requested our intervention. We felt it was not our function to encroach upon normal union prerogatives, such as in enforcing the collective agreement.

Our third resolve was to immerse ourselves as much as possible in day-to-day union activity in terms of grievances, safety problems, evaluation, etc. Brother McCandlish is a job steward and chairman of the sawmill grievance committee, and in my own case, I act as the vice-chairman of the plywood grievance committee and plywood evaluation committee member.

We involve ourselves in order to keep our roots and to remain in touch with the day-to-day problems of workers. We felt we could thereby more ably bring the workers' experience into the board room, the expression of which we considered the important essence of our function.

As our terms as directors are indefinite, we sought to establish yearly votes of confidence in ourselves by seeking our successful nomination and election to these types of representative committees.

The failure of a worker-director to be involved in such a fashion because of his constant contact with management, and issues of a much larger scale, could possibly lead to that director's feeling very important and possibly even his forgetting the many issues and problems that still exist for workers on the shop floor. In my own case as a job steward representing workers during grievances and during disciplinary action, I am reminded frequently that workers can still be treated in an arbitrary manner by management, contrary to what we as trade unionists consider a worker's basic rights.

We finally decided also to ensure that workers had the opportunity to question us about decisions made at the board level and to give regular directors' reports at our monthly union meetings.

We have found these guidelines effective in maintaining our credibility.

Has the appointment of two workers to the Board of Directors of Kootenay Forest Products affected the situation there, and how does management perceive Kootenay Forest Products' present situation? Quoting Jack Sigalet, Kootenay Forest Products' plant manager: "The people of Nelson have been kicked in the teeth by outsiders and this accounts for Kootenay Forest Products having developed the reputation as the wildest labour plant in British Columbia."

Again quoting Jack Sigalet from a recent speech: "Kootenay Forest Products was the classic example of an absentee-owned corporation. Forward planning was perpetually discarded by the owners and day-to-day decisions were continued on a hand-to-mouth basis until the company was sold. Our woodlands were virtually a tragedy, our plants were run down, our equipment was not maintained, our cash reserves were negative and our inventories were gutted of all usable material. Since then we have had some changes and improvements. The two hourly directors have made substantial contributions to the operation. The sawmill has had $1,500,000 worth of improvements; Woodlands has spent several million dollars on roads, we have a new $300,000 logging camp at Duncan Lake and most important we have improved our productivity in 1976 over 1975 by 100% in lumber and 20% in plywood. Not the least part of this improvement can be attributed to the people at all levels involved, sales, supervision, clerical and hourly—all have contributed."

In short, from management's point of view, productivity has increased, morale has improved, operations are more efficient, wildcats are down, and profits are up. What, then, have been the tangible results for workers as a result of their participation at the board level?

As a result of Kootenay Forest Products' transformation into a viable entity, the workers' jobs are now secure. Workers of Kootenay Forest

Products now have the right and opportunity to review, criticize, and make suggestions in respect to planned renovations, installations of new equipment, or changes in production flow. Plans for the $1,500,000 sawmill renovations, for example, were made available to the workers who made recommendations, some of which lightened their work load. Significant changes to the original plans were implemented as a result of worker input. Morale, safety, and production have improved significantly as a result.

The historical tenuous viability of Kootenay Forest Products has created a continuing interest by workers in the economic performance of the company. Thus we as worker-directors take our monthly financial statements to the union meetings, giving everyone the opportunity to know what the economic realities of Kootenay Forest Products are at the time. Today any worker can request and receive from management the audited annual financial statements of the company. As directors representing workers, we consider this a major achievement, particularly because the first problem we encountered in our new function was the issue of confidentiality. Boards of directors normally function in a milieu of relative secrecy, and we initially were expected to follow suit and refrain from divulging board business outside of the boardroom. We were thus in the untenable position of attempting to be representative of and accountable to workers without owning the right to report to them. We sought legal advice from our local union, the international union, and government officials, and after some negotiations we attained the right to divulge all information to the workers at our own discretion, excluding, of course, financial matters relating to any potential speculation.

At one time at Kootenay Forest Products, management maintained personnel files about its employees, the contents of which were not available to workers. The union and the workers considered this a serious problem, but were unable to resolve the situation through the grievance procedure. The union approached us and we placed the personnel-file matter on the agenda of a Board of Directors meeting. As a consequence, today every employee has the right to examine his personnel file and thus has the opportunity to challenge an incorrect entry. This right can help the union in enforcing the collective agreement.

Many workers had also felt that the company-products discount for employees should have been increased. As directors we had the right to examine the financial statements of our retail yard and thus argue successfully that the financial impact on the company of a 25 percent discount for employees was negligible.

An item that had angered workers, particularly under the ownership of Eddy Match, was the fact that workers had often been laid off with little or no advance warning. Once again through the Board of Directors we achieved the right to a two-week advance notice for any impending layoff. Workers now at least have some lead time to prepare in terms of unemployment insurance, etc. Upon occasion, as a result of our knowledge about future planning, we have been able to effect the startup of an extra shift in a different department or even initiate an early execution of a planned capital expenditure in order to provide alternative work for employees scheduled for layoff. In one instance we were able to reduce a planned layoff of 60 workers to only 10.

As the result of an inspection tour of our operation by a government safety inspector, the Board of Kootenay Forest Products was faced with approving a safety and hygiene-related expenditure in excess of $100,000. In our province, fines for violations of government safety orders are often negligible. That was a factor, we suspect, in the apparent reluctance by some of the directors in approving a large capital expenditure for such a purpose. The presence of worker-directors on our board ensured the approval of that expenditure.

Many grievances with serious labor-relations overtones have been solved as a result of a dramatic improvement of communications at Kootenay Forest Products. In the past we found that conflicts, particularly labor relations issues, were often stalled and hung up within middle management. Issues had been left dangling without top management being aware of the gravity or full details of a serious problem. Our presence and our ability to communicate with top-level management, as directors, has encouraged a better communications flow.

In October 1975 the President of Kootenay Forest Products changed, and as worker-directors, we had some input into that appointment. Because Jack Sigalet, the chosen manager, has some relatively progressive ideas, our input into that change has indirectly facilitated a more flexible approach to management-labor relations, better communications between levels of management, the utilization of talent, and improved employee morale.

These, then, have been some of the positive results for workers at Kootenay Forest Products.

The entire question of industrial democracy has only recently become a serious topic of interest in Canada, and concrete examples thereof in a Canadian context are rare. Therefore it might be useful to examine some basic questions about worker participation from the perspective of the Kootenay Forest Products experiment.

The experiment at Kootenay Forest Products is taking place in a factory setting, and the work is basically structured in line with Frederick Taylor's scientific-management model. Any conclusions drawn from our experience have to be qualified by taking that fact into consideration.

Question No. 1: Has the experiment at Kootenay Forest Products encountered any problems?

Yes, as a result of having more information and input through their representative on the Board of Directors, many workers have developed an increasing interest in how their immediate job relates to the total operation and how it could be humanized. Workers thus requested the opportunity to operate one key production area by themselves. This proposed six-month experiment was perceived to be a threat by the supervisors, who felt their jobs to be on the line. Friction was created between workers and first-line supervisors as a result of the supervisors' active opposition and resistance to the experiment.

The experiment did proceed, but, unfortunately, two weeks later all supervisors walked out over an internal management dispute. In that context top management felt it necessary to stop the experiment, a decision that disappointed the workers. During the supervisors' wildcat, workers remained on the job and successfully operated the entire plant with no supervisors for a day and a half, even increasing productivity in one section of the mill.

Because worker-directors have increased input and access to information, supervisors have, upon occasion, appeared to have their noses out of joint. During their wildcat strike, supervisors requested their own representation on the Board of Directors. Perhaps their presence on the board has legitimized for the supervisors their latent desire for more input and information.

Question No. 2: Has the experiment at Kootenay Forest Products reinforced or negated the rationale for implementing a form of industrial democracy here in Canada?

From my own personal experience I believe that the need for a worker's control over his or her working life is a deep and enduring trait. Present work and management structures fail miserably in filling that need. In fact, much research indicates that traditional work structures harm workers and are making them ugly. The Kootenay Forest Products experience has been a positive one and leads us to believe that industrial democracy has the potential of creating a working environment worthy of the motivation and spirit that workers initially bring to their task. Placing labels aside, we feel that the time has come for a fundamental change in the way that work is organized.

Question No. 3: Does that fundamental change entail the placement of two workers on the Board of Directors of a company?

The drive to place two workers on the Board of Directors of Kootenay Forest Products was not the result of any preconceived notions about industrial democracy, but the outgrowth of a search for answers for a number of specific company problems. The two worker-directors were never considered the final solution to worker alienation or a definite requirement of industrial democracy. In our view a legitimate form of industrial democracy has to extend some meaningful decision-making authority right down to workers on the shop floor. At Kootenay Forest Products we have demonstrated some of the benefits of board room worker participation, both for management and for workers. Beyond that, however, we are attempting to evolve from the bottom up a form of participation or industrial democracy suited to our own circumstances. The union would like to pursue an experiment in self-determination and operate a key production area without any supervision. It is our impression that workers, particularly in our industry, are over-supervised and that this excessive baby-sitting of workers is both totally unnecessary and completely counterproductive. This type of experiment could involve workers in a meaningful way, providing opportunities for exercising real authority and for collective decision making. The success of the experiment, of course, would be measured by management in terms of quality and quantity of production. The workers would define success in terms of such potential indicators of reduced levels of work alienation, expressed as an increased sense of freedom, fewer grievances, greater work satisfaction, less sickness, and fewer accidents.

Basically we feel that worker-directors are of great benefit even in isolation, but as only one aspect of industrial democracy. They should be coupled with a shop floor worker participation structure. The formation of such a day-to-day participatory structure has to be guided above all by workers, and consequently worker-directors should pay an essential role in ensuring an appropriate structure.

Question No. 4: Does the presence of two worker-directors on a Board of Directors impede the effective functioning of that board?

No, the relationship of our directors is a cordial one. We have a diverse group representing all kinds of political viewpoints. Ray Williston, the chairman of our board, is an ex-Social Credit cabinet minister, and I am an active member of the New Democratic Party, yet we find that we can respect our differences, put them aside, and perform our function efficiently.

Differences of opinion do arise at times, of course; nevertheless, our relationship has progressed from initially two workers with a slight chip on their shoulders, facing a polite condescendence from management board members, to a healthy respect for each other.

Question No. 5: Has the experiment at Kootenay Forest Products compromised or harmed the interests of the union?

No, Kootenay Forest Products is still noted for its militant work force, and a strong union presence is apparent on the shop floor. In our opinion, instituting a proper and successful form of industrial democracy presumes a strong union presence. A union's involvement with a cooperative and democratic organization and the union's concern with the dignity of labor are vital to the success of industrial democracy.

Enforcing the collective agreement and negotiating improved wages and conditions remain the prerogative of the union. During previous negotiations, Kootenay Forest Products workers, in line with their tradition, voted for one of the highest strike votes in the B. C. interior. We have also had one wildcat strike under our previous manager in which both worker-directors participated.

Certainly in terms of the obvious traditional indicators of a union's militancy, the union at Kootenay Forest Products has not been adversely affected.

Question No. 6: Does the initial success at Kootenay Forest Products in reducing labor unrest and in improving productivity call for the importation of the European model of industrial democracy, such as West German codetermination, to Canada?

Industrial democracy implies from our point of view the full participation of the worker in shaping and creating a participatory structure in tune with the Canadian realities. As such, industrial democracy has to be an evolutionary phenomenon. We do not, therefore, deem it advisable to transfer holus-bolus a structure such as codetermination to either British Columbia or Alberta. We think it would fail.

Any attempt to implement industrial democracy based solely on the rationale of reducing strikes and increasing productivity will likely also fail, since workers will almost certainly consider such an approach as a manipulation. Increased productivity, reduced absenteeism, fewer wildcat strikes, and the like will be a spin-off benefit from industrial democracy only if an honest commitment is made to give workers enough authority for meaningful decision making and in seriously modifying some of the destructive aspects of scientific and autocratic management.

It is my belief that management and society in general have to face up to the unarticulated rejection of autocratic work structures, particularly by the young and well-informed workers. Failure to do so will undoubtedly increase the number of wildcats and other primal explosions resulting from worker frustrations.

On the other hand, I think unions will have to start leading the fight against worker alienation, or increasingly they will be considered irrelevant by the younger worker. If unions do not rapidly become aware of all the issues relating to worker participation, they might very well find the cards stacked against them if governments, through legislative action, or managements, by unilateral action, attempt to impose a bastardized form of "industrial democracy" on workers.

In conclusion, I would like to say that we at Kootenay Forest Products welcome this type of conference. We feel that the concept of industrial democracy has come of age in Canada. It is one of the most important and most exciting issues facing both labor and management today. At Kootenay Forest Products in Nelson, we are accepting and looking forward to that challenge.

Index